Death, Taxes
&
Procurement

Death, Taxes & Procurement

An effective, novel approach to selling your products or services to the biggest customer in the world: the United States Federal Government.

An approach from the viewpoint of private enterprise rather than all of the data from the government, which tends to be just a little biased.

Robert D. Horejsh

iUniverse, Inc.
New York Lincoln Shanghai

Death, Taxes & Procurement

Copyright © 2007 by Robert D. Horejsh

iUniverse books may be ordered through booksellers or by contacting:

iUniverse
2021 Pine Lake Road, Suite 100
Lincoln, NE 68512
www.iuniverse.com
1-800-Authors (1-800-288-4677)

Because of the dynamic nature of the Internet, any Web addresses or links contained in this book may have changed since publication and may no longer be valid.

The views expressed in this work are solely those of the author and do not necessarily reflect the views of the publisher, and the publisher hereby disclaims any responsibility for them.

ISBN: 978-0-595-44921-7 (pbk)
ISBN: 978-0-595-89244-0 (ebk)

Printed in the United States of America

Contents

Acknowledgements

Death, Taxes & Procurement is an amalgam of information gleaned from a variety of public websites, training seminars and personal experiences. Specific information sources are noted in the story and blog information, which is usually noted plus the author's opinions, should probably be taken with a grain of salt.

Quotations are from *The Oxford Dictionary Of Quotations, Third Edition*.

Definitions, Acronyms and Abbreviations are from various public resources including government agencies' websites and government training data. The Defense Acquisition University (DAU) *Glossary of Defense Acquisition Acronyms & Terms* is a helpful source.

Current news and data came from regular public sources: newspapers, public radio and television broadcasts.

Computer assistance was from www.budgethomepage.com

Moral support and typing assistance from my lovely wife, Mary.

Thank you.

Foreword

Benjamin Franklin, the great early American pundit, was commenting on the inevitability of certain things to which I've added "Procurement" to "Death and Taxes." Procurement by the United States Federal Government is also inevitable because they are, and will most likely remain, the largest user of goods and services in the world.

This book is a basic guide to selling to the federal government in more of a prose style in an effort to make it hopefully somewhat interesting. Not to say that the subject of selling to the government is totally dull reading but until you're actively experiencing the methods, much of it is hard to connect the necessary steps.

The steps are actually logical if followed because the government has genuinely made an effort to simplify the process. Even though there's a lot of information to consider, not all of it is necessary to get started. This book provides the reader with background information and the initial tools to decide if this potentially lucrative market is for you.

Literary license has been taken in the obvious fiction aspect of the story although the facts of the "how-to" manual contained herein are as current as possible. The author does not take responsibility for any errors or out-dated material in this book. The author is not engaged in rendering legal or accounting advice and suggests using the services of a competent professional in said issues. The author does not guarantee the reader will secure a contract and is not responsible for any costs incurred while pursuing governmental business. Regarding the fictional aspect of this book, any resemblance to actual people, companies or events is purely coincidental. That's right, this book is nonfiction except for those parts that aren't.

Enjoy the book and I wish you success in your endeavors. Your patience and persistence cannot be stressed enough when pursuing government contracts. Without patience and persistence, your chances of success are greatly diminished unless you are one lucky person.

Incidentally, there is no such thing as luck.

Robert D. Horejsh

1

The Story

"I hate owning my own business!" Bill nearly shouted at poor Jeremy, his production supervisor. Jeremy didn't even flinch at the outburst because he knew Bill was, as usual, just stressed out over their tight production schedules. Jeremy did a quick about face and headed out the door back to the shop.

Techno-Systems, Inc. and its owner were on the edge. Today's big issue was the same as yesterdays' and most likely the same as tomorrows', they needed a healthy shot of new customers to hopefully balance out their backlog.

Bill Nelson, was in his early forties, almost 6' tall and maybe 10 lbs. overweight. He was a neat dresser although his usually stylish look was disrupted by his habit of wearing prescription safety glasses with side shields all of the time, even while away from work. His clothing of choice was blue denim shirts with the company logo over slacks, never jeans. When the occasion called for a suit and tie, the nerdy glasses stayed.

Bill, the owner of Techno-Systems, Inc. for the last 15 months, literally scratched his head and thought about the problem. He had enough work scheduled for maybe 30 days and then zilch. Not exactly a comforting feeling. That was just one of the problems of owning your own company; when business is going good you're on top of the world but when business goes south, you take it to bed with you every night.

Oh sure, something would come in like it always seemed to at the last minute because that's the way his customers were. They just expected his quick turnaround time on their needs without a lot of sympathy for what it did to his production. Bill's quality inspector, Kevin, advised him to be patient and the problem would work itself out. He also added that it would take a long time, "sort of like being kicked to death by a rabbit."

Then Bill had subtly suggested to his biggest customer that orders placed a little in advance would really help, but he didn't want to rock the boat, mainly because of a potentially damaging development in their specific market.

Techno-Systems had started losing some of their more stable customers almost a year ago when his old boss became his new competitor. What happened was the original owner and founder of Techno-Systems, Dennis Bell, who ran the company for over eleven years, was caught messing around with a woman other than his wife. Patty, the jilted wife, filed for divorce and decided to go after what would hurt Dennis the most, Techno-Systems, Inc. She should have been more conventional and settled for the house although the sense of revenge felt good at the time.

Patty did her best but she was in over her head and as soon as Dennis had satisfied a too short, in hindsight, non-compete clause, he started a new company. Patty had heard the scuttlebutt about the new company and approached Bill, her plant manager at the time with a deal he couldn't refuse. After a brief negotiation, Bill closed on the deal making him the latest proud owner of Techno-Systems, Inc.

It seemed a little suspicious that Dennis hadn't fought harder to keep his company during the divorce proceedings as he had loved Techno-Systems but it now looked as though he had improved his position with the change. Talk about turning a "crisis into a creative opportunity." Dennis was now able to buy new equipment with the most current technology and pirated eight of the better employees from his old company. It didn't take long before some of Bill's customers also began drifting over to become Dennis' customers.

Even with Dennis cherry-picking Bill's customer base, Bill felt confident he could pick up a bunch of new customers himself to replace them. He managed to talk a few of his old customers into giving him another chance though it didn't feel like a long term solution. Under the best of circumstances, new business is said to be the lifeblood of any business and the current conditions were certainly not the best. Bill really needed a stable base of customers with ideally realistic longer lead-time requirements. So the bottom line was, he needed both short and long lead-time, any and all, types of new customers.

Bill's first step was to analyze his situation and come up with a plan. He knew he would gladly accept any reasonable business but he also knew that he couldn't continue working on his present basis. Ideally he would keep the customers he could and add as many new ones as possible. He vowed to himself to always look for new business even after he improved his present position because the best time to take on new accounts was when you didn't need them so badly.

When you're under the gun your options are stifled by a sense of desperation and you're forced to do what ever you have to do. Bill still had twenty-two fulltime employees and three part-time to keep busy. He was genuinely concerned for their individual welfare even though he knew he had to take care of the company first so that they would have a place to earn a living. This was the first time Bill was totally responsible for so many people and he took that responsibility quite seriously. In addition, these days good employees were hard to find, and losing them after they were trained and effective only to have to train new ones with unknown issues was a bad situation.

Bill thought a plan with long-range goals with short-range goals to support them was the way to go. Twelve years ago, before starting at Techno-Systems, Bill had worked for a company that supplied machined product to the United States Federal Government and had good memories of those days. Sure, they had worked under a rigid time schedule to complete specific processes but the overall longer lead times allowed for better and more effective planning. He remembered his old bosses complaining about getting paid on time but he had also heard since then about a new payment system mandated to pay in thirty days, even shorter under certain prearranged terms.

The fact was, in addition to being the world's biggest customer, the federal government also has the best credit rating despite their huge debt. By law, federal procurements must be paid for within 30 days of when that payment is approved. Funds are usually deposited electronically to a vendor's bank account. And given the speed and lack of float, the effective period is really closer to 14 days.

Bill had always considered getting a government contract almost on par with finding the Holy Grail and knew that somewhere between that and all of the bad rumors he had heard about contracting was a middle ground. Maybe part of his solution could be found there but he really didn't have the time to pursue it now. Maybe later. The fact is: doing business with the government is not for struggling companies and if a company is in trouble, trying to fulfill government contract can pull them under.

A case in point was a small Midwestern machine shop doing around a million dollars a year in commercial receivables when they decided to get into government contracting. They hired a person to search for contracts, process the paperwork and submit the invoices though they never quite got to the invoicing part. Having cash flow problems forced the company into putting the government orders back because they had to do the quick turnaround jobs to pay their bills. The first year they captured a million dollars worth of government business in eight different orders of varying amounts. Inaccurate progress reports put them in a false sense of security until they missed the first shipment. They never recovered and went out of business.

The company had had a goal but they didn't have a plan. Their initial goal was to eventually have two-million dollars of commercial business and two-million dollars of government business with appropriate lead times for both. Without a plan and enough resources to weather the ongoing operational expenses, they became overwhelmed and all parties concerned lost. In part due to the large purchase of forgings to machine for two of the government jobs, they couldn't even afford to file under a reorganization plan because they were too far gone in debt.

Bill's first priority was to find the most business in the shortest amount of time then he would look into what the government had to offer when everything settled down. For right now, he would stay in the more familiar territory of commercial work and started by ordering the most current publication of his state's manufacturer's directory. There were options for tools for marketing but Bill stuck with a hard copy of the directory and a CD with the same data for his laptop. There were a few accounts that had so much potential that everyone pursued them and so would he, but he'd also try to pick the low hanging fruit closest to home.

There were a few marketing strategies Bill was familiar with but at this time, he was trying to decide whether to go after business like a rifle or a shotgun. The rifle approach was to have a clear target and take shots at specific accounts. The shotgun approach was to scatter his efforts at a wider range of accounts and hope for a hit. Either/or a combination of both would probably put something on his plate.

Government business was said to be a moving target and it was true that its market changed often. No doubt about it, thought Bill. My best shot will be something I'm familiar with for now and to pursue commercial business to satisfy our immediate hunger. I'll go big-game government hunting when the pressure is off to bring in faster turnaround type business but for now, the rifle and commercial approach was the way for him to go.

A regular old roadmap was Bill's primary logistics tool and he spread it open on his desk. It was a way to refresh his marketing mind as to the areas he had been mentally overlooking when he thought of new business. After referring to the directory for the cities and counties within easy driving distance, his plan began to take shape. Bill thought, how come I didn't know all of this for so long? It must be the "forest for the trees" syndrome sort of thing.

Bill liked physical aids like roadmaps, directories and dictionaries. It must have satisfied a traditionalist's need he had or maybe it was like comfort food but he had obtained a government dictionary, definitions of terms used in contracting, and perused a few words related to his future quest to tide him over while he firmed up his commercial business. This term caught his eye:

Acquisition: Process of purchasing goods and services (including construction) for the use of a governmental activity through purchase, rent, or lease. Includes the establishment of needs, description of requirements, selection of procurement method, selection of sources, solicitation of procurement, solicitation for offers, award of contract, financing, contraction administration, and related functions.

Acquisition, that's what Bill wanted Techno-Systems to be a part of in the future. Six months later the situation looked a lot better on the commercial front and he was ready to attack the federal government market. Bill had a positive attitude about this interesting adventure because, as he liked to say: "No sense being pessimistic. It wouldn't work anyway."

Bill's sense of humor had changed over the years he had been with Techno-Systems in large part because of being around Kevin and Jeremy. Kevin had a fairly good, if not well-used, joke for every occasion but Jeremy had a biting, sarcastic bit of wisdom always on the tip of his tongue, although he usually kept it to himself. When the situation merited it, Jeremy would make some of the most profound statements with a totally straight face and Bill would sometimes have to ponder what Jeremy had said to understand the full meaning.

As part of Techno-Systems' brain pool, Kevin and Jeremy would be big factors in Bill's endeavor to do business with the federal government. He knew from first hand experience that the owners and managers of a company were not necessarily the best minds of the company even though they might have the most business acumen. Bill would utilize all of his assets and do it right the first time.

2

Getting Started

"Bambi, if the fresh coffee is ready, would you mind getting me a cup?" Bill normally got his own coffee but he had already checked the coffee machine twice waiting for the morning's Swedish speed. "Sure Mister Nelson, I'd love to," Bambi called back. Honest to God, Bambi was her legal first name and it fit her with those big doe-eyes. For the first few weeks she worked at Techno-Systems she was somewhat of a distraction for everyone though things had settled down by now. "Thanks" Bill said and settled down himself to ponder the federal government marketplace.

In the time that had passed since Bill had planned his commercial account's blitz, he had enjoyed pretty fair success in his efforts. In fact, his success in chartered territory had buoyed his confidence in his present endeavor, the government. Bill owed a good deal of that success to his motto of "plan your work, work your plan" philosophy. Now he would apply some of those same techniques to the government market. It was time to get started by doing some basic research.

The government has been buying, or contracting, goods and services since 1776, when George Washington asked Philip J. Schuyler to buy arms from Major Duncan at Schenectady. Today, the Department of Defense budget alone is *453 billion dollars*. That 453 billion does not include spending on current Afghan and Iraq wars($100 billion) and proposed Homeland Security funding of ($41.1 billion) or a grand total of almost *$600,000,000,000.00*.

We, as a nation, hear and read about billions of dollars so often that we have become inured to the term "billions" and take it for granted. Here's how much a billion really is:

- One billion seconds ago it was the year 1975.

- One billion minutes ago Jesus Christ walked the face of the earth.

- One billion pennies stacked flat on each other would be almost 1,000 miles high. The Space Shuttle orbits the earth at 225 miles high.

- One billion dollars laid end to end would encircle the earth almost four times.

- One billion dollars to the U.S. Government is less than eight hours worth of spending.

It's true, a billion really is a lot and then consider a trillion being a thousand billion. The point is that a drop in the bucket for the government is like a tsunami to a small business. The practice of the huge, suspiciously no-bid contracts being awarded to a handful of big businesses is losing support by the real backbone of this great country, all of the smaller businesses and the general public. The trend seems to be going back to "Buy American" and buy smaller to ensure this greatness.

What does the United States Federal Government buy? Everything! They buy, rent or lease absolutely everything, everyday from someone. From one person operations and up, almost every company has something to sell to the United States Government. People are only limited by their imaginations and an unwarranted fear of working with such a huge entity. If they insist on spending the money you've been paying them in taxes, you might as well see if you can get any of it back by selling products or services to them. If not you, someone else will provide that product or service and make fair money doing it.

The government, in many respects, has genuinely made an effort to make it easier to do business with all of the various agencies that comprise the federal government. Try to picture the federal government as being made up of agencies made up of more specific groups made up of people. Of those people, an individual person may be the only one you will be dealing with if you get a contract. Looking at the United States Federal

Government as a whole is naturally intimidating and thinking about all of the scary rumors regarding it doesn't help either.

Well, Bill thought, I'm past the scary part because I've seen it done and I know I can do it. Even he was surprised by the numbers though and the thought that such a small percentage of business by government standards could have such a large impact on his company. His next step was to make a plan to start looking at open business available to bid on. He knew what he thought he knew but he didn't know what he didn't know. After clearing his mind of that confusing revelation, he decided to call his local Procurement Technical Assistance Center, or PTAC, to see what they might have to offer.

Before he telephoned them though he decided it would probably be better to investigate a little on his own by doing a search on his computer. We live in the information age and it's always better to see what background can be discerned before even bothering a person and waste everybody's time while looking foolish by asking obvious questions. Not knowing the basic answers or being confused with obvious jargon can be more than embarrassing, it can shake the confidence of the person you're talking to and create a bad first impression.

Another positive factor is the ability of most people to more easily remember information they've had to work on a little bit. More *stuff* is retained if you question yourself before questioning someone else. With that in mind, Bill reached the website directing him to the PTAC website in his state. He found out the local PTAC wasn't very local being almost 200 miles away. Oh well, he thought, with today's communications it doesn't really matter unless I have a need to see them in person.

At the "local" website, Bill discovered an offering of seminars on subjects from the very basics to more specific topics. A few testimonials convinced him that the seminars were effective but the next basic seminar wasn't scheduled for two months and Bill was chomping at the bit to get going. Bill had another interesting thought of bringing his old boss, Patti, to help collect and submit any necessary data.

The benefits of this idea were twofold because Patti had kept the books for Dennis and as the manager after the divorce she knew the inner-workings of Techno-Systems. Another positive was, even though Patti was his "old" boss, she was actually only in her mid-thirties and a real fox in Bill's eyes. Which was another plus because Bill had had a crush on Patti ever since he started working at Techno-Systems and sensed that Patti kind of liked him back. The entire company seemed to know about Dennis' escapades with women other than Patti because of Dennis' big mouth. It had always seemed to Bill that Dennis had wanted his indiscretions in the open and welcomed the divorce and subsequent settlement.

Denny's loss could be my gain, mused Bill as he punched in Patti's telephone number.

"I'd be delighted to work with you," Patti said, but it was more the way she said it that made Bill so happy with his decision to call her. She was going to stop by the company the day after tomorrow and discuss the possibilities of teaming up. It had probably been a little boring, just sitting around her apartment most likely thinking about the house she had passed up for the vengeful Techno-Systems settlement. She and Dennis had not had children so there was no good reason to just stay home.

Patti was about 5' 7" tall and, particularly to Bill, had a nice body. She wasn't voluptuous but that wasn't Bill's idea of the ideal look and preferred the trim, healthy appearance that Patty had. She had strawberry blond hair, wavy to the extent of almost kinky, worn medium length and always looked neat however she was dressed, casual or more formal. Bill couldn't help but envision her every time her name came up, even just talking to her on the telephone conjured up her image.

Bill got back to his computer search for government procurement information. He discovered a lot of government purchasing besides the federal government. The state, his and all the other ones, universities, hospitals, colleges, counties, cities, school districts, road districts, etc., the list went on and on. This was besides all of the large and small agencies under the federal umbrella plus, any non-profit agency that spends grant money on behalf of a government entity was fair game. Counting all of them, there are over 80,000 governmental markets, although Bill was thinking Department of Defense (DoD).

There is also a trend to privatize many of the jobs previously performed by the government. Opportunities for companies to actually replace lesser agencies are becoming commonplace in an effort to reduce government spending. Some could argue the apparent increased efficiency of the private sector over the public sector in most instances is true. It's not easy being the largest consumer in the world in terms of both dollars spent and sheer diversity of needs; things fall through the cracks and become perceived or actual government inefficiencies.

The government has stated: "in a democratic free enterprise system, the government should not compete with its citizens" and adds that "it has been and continues to be the general policy of the government to rely on competitive private enterprise to supply products and services it needs." These policy precepts emphasize that where private sources are available, they should be "looked at first" to provide the commercial and industrial goods and services that the government needs; that some functions are "inherently government in nature" and should be performed by federal employees; and that, where private performance is feasible, "rigorous cost comparison should be used to determine where the work is to be done." It has been many years since the above statement was made and since then the philosophy has been drifting steadily towards private enterprise.

Bill read that only about two-percent of small businesses are engaged in this lucrative trade even though it is open to many, many more. Why do so many companies allow so many billions of dollars bypass them? First, they never take the time to explore the federal marketplace because of unfounded and blown-up rumors they've heard about the trials of contracting. Second, the paperwork and detail work seems overwhelming. Third, past performance requirements appear to be a "catch 22" because if you can't get a first order, how can you build a history? Fourth, they never even try. Fifth, they made a half-hearted effort to try, failed, and gave up

Bill read on to debunk those issues:

1. A lot has changed and it's easy now and more transparent to go to any computer to search for not only the opportunities but also what's needed to bid on them.

2. True, there are a lot of details although they've been simplified and most of the "paperwork" can actually be done paperless over the computer.

3. Besides being able to refer to a solid commercial business history, the Small Business Administration, or SBA, can guide a company through programs to turn a perceived disadvantage into an advantage.

4. Try.

5. Try again.

Wondering if he had any mandated advantages in his situation, Bill read on. For if you are a small company, as designated by the government, you join the ranks of almost eighty percent of the companies in this country. The SBA will give you up-to-date information on what determines a disadvantaged company and what your status is currently. Some larger companies have been caught misguiding the government by claiming their companies were smaller than they actually were. One of the benefits of having a special status such as being designated disadvantaged, woman-owned, veteran-owned, service-disabled owned, minority-owned or in a Historically Underutilized Business Zone, or HUB Zone, is that bids may be ten percent higher than competing bids from a larger "advantaged" business. In theory, these offsets may be cumulative, if not always for pricing enhancement, certainly for the determination of award.

The Procurement Technical Assistance Centers and the Small Business Administration were there to help people like Bill and he intended to take full advantage of their services. After all, he did pay in the tax money that ultimately paid for their existence and he was to find out that they truly were helpful.

Without waiting any longer, Bill called the SBA and set up an appointment to speak to a specialist as soon as they were available, maybe within two weeks. Bill was really feeling like he was learning a lot of background and getting off to a good start. Since he had to wait a while before the next scheduled PTAC seminar on the basics of selling to the government, Bill decided to look into getting registered himself. He was also to find that all of what he learned on his own would make everything clearer, faster when he finally attended the first seminar because he was already more knowledgeable.

Bill decided to write a Mission Statement before he spoke to the SBA because other successful companies all seemed to have one. As usual, his internet searches didn't disappoint him with all sorts of hits, but the best he found on the subject was from a blog. The writer of the blog suggested taking your time, look at other Mission Statements but *do not* copy them and make sure you're writing a mission and *not* goals. The statement should be less than 30 seconds long, a cross between an executive summary and a slogan. Other suggestions included:

- A Mission Statement should say who your company is, what you do, what you stand for, and why you do it.

- An effective Mission Statement is best when developed with input from all the members of an organization.

- The best ones are only 3-4 sentences long.

- Avoid saying how great you are, what great quality and great services you provide.

- Using other companies' Mission Statements for concept only, not verbatim.

- Be honest and realistic as customers will recognize B.S.

Okay, thought Bill. He normally wasn't big on company meetings because he had never liked public speaking and had too many other things going on right now to learn how. Besides company meetings were disruptive in time and cost money so he'd pass out a note with the next paycheck instead.

Patti was the most likely candidate for registering Techno-Systems with the various agencies or whatever because she had actually run the company for awhile. She had the inside workings down pat and her accuracy in writing was almost obsessive as anyone who had had to retype her reports and letters already knew. Yes, Patti would be perfect.

3

Getting Registered

"Patti!" cried Mary, the receptionist at Techno-Systems and still a good friend of her old boss. "What are you doing here, do you have time for lunch?"

"Hi Mary, no lunch, I'm here to see Bill. Didn't Bill say anything about me coming?" "Uh-uh," said Mary, shaking her head, "but it's great to see you, you've been a stranger lately."

Patti decided not to mention her reason for seeing Bill just in case she didn't end up working there again.

"Mr. Nelson, Patti Bell is here to see you."

Bill said he'd be right out. Bill insisted on the office being more formal than when Denny or Patti were in charge because the way things were going, he was starting to envision a bigger, more professional company. In his opinion, when people acted more professional, they became more professional.

"Hello, Patti, come on in." Bill shook Patti's hand and asked if she'd like a cup of coffee. They had a pleasant conversation, Bill explained what he wanted to do, made an offer, Patti accepted and would start tomorrow, Friday the 15th, the start of a new pay period. That was easy, thought Bill, and took it as a good sign of things to come.

Not everyone was overjoyed by Patti's return however. Jeremy, Techno-Systems Production Supervisor who had replaced Bill when Bill moved-up to ownership from manufacturing, still harbored animosity toward Patti. She had been a grade A bitch to Jeremy, a machine operator during the short time Patti had been in charge by questioning Jeremy's competence. Patti tried to push everything through the shop by sheer willpower without any regard to basic manufacturing knowledge and Jeremy had felt

15

picked on. Bill was aware of Patti's unrealistic tirades and actually agreed with the general consensus that Patti should have stayed the hell out of manufacturing. Jeremy always took the verbal abuse with an almost scarily calm demeanor though and the news of Patti's return was treated with the same feeling of quiet resolve.

The next morning, after the immediate fires were put out, Pat and Bill had their first real planning meeting. Bill handed over the pertinent information he had compiled so far and set Patti up with a complete working cubicle just outside his office. He wanted her nearby but didn't want to give anyone the impression of her being his secretary, or for that matter, back in her old position as management either.

Pretty much everything pointed to the first step as getting Techno-Systems registered with the Central Contractor Registration site on the internet. After a quick search on the initials "CCR" and a few minutes of perusing the more popular hits, Patti settled on the most prominent at www.ccr.gov. Search engines always produced more hits than a person could think imaginable on any one subject and a minute or two checking a few of them out usually yielded interesting information. Patti found a lot of specific website addresses might have changed although search engines always worked.

The Central Contractor Registration site had links to other sites for the initial information she needed for registration besides contact links for after she was registered. Patti was to find that all the different government websites were very friendly to work with and designed to be easy to navigate for even the most novice visitor. Any readers necessary for different computers to communicate were available for free download so just about anyone could access any information without having to buy anything. Patti was computer savvy now but even she had been tricked into buying things she didn't need by unscrupulous private websites a few years ago. Her rule of thumb was to never give out a credit card number and found that none were needed for any legitimate government website.

The check list that Patti made looked like this:
CCR registration-

1. Need DUNS #

2. Need TIN #

3. 9 digit zip code #

4. Business starting date?

5. Fiscal year ends?

6. SBA status?

7. NAICS code #s 6 digit

8. SIC code #s 4 digit

9. PSC, FSC code #s

10. Financial info—ABA routing #, account #, Automated Clearing House

"Good Grief!" said Patti out loud to no one in particular.

Patti could have saved a little time by printing out a "CCR Registration Worksheet" but at least she had the right idea. Because to start filling out the registration form over the internet without some advance homework would have meant stopping and saving a lot during the process. Even if she compiled most everything on her list beforehand, she'd still probably forget something. That was okay though as long as she minimized having to pause to research a subject.

The CCR website also had handbooks and other reference material Patti could read and/or printout. Whatever tools she utilized, the most important part was the honesty and accuracy she reflected in her data presented. And as complicated as this first step seemed, it really didn't take long because Patti was organized and had planned in advance. Patti and Bill were to learn the simple secret to starting any seemingly big complex project and having the "stick-to-itiveness" to finish was: "How does one eat an elephant? One bite at a time."

The most daunting endeavor could be accomplished by breaking it down to its most basic steps: "A thousand mile journey begins with a single step. "A more current slogan from a popular sporting goods manufacturer isn't too bad either: "Just do it. "Which is what they did.

Bill gave Patti a BIG tip earlier. "Big" (his emphasis) because it would save everyone involved a lot of time in the future. Bill sent a memo for everyone to note all of the identification names and phrases and all of the passwords they might use or initiate and give the information to Patti. She would consolidate them and compile a confidential master list for Bill and her only. If everyone just jotted down whatever they had on a scrap of paper or figure they'd just remember it, they would most likely lose it, forget it or be unavailable if someone else needed it. The master list would end up being quite long and prove to be handy later.

Techno-Systems had been around for a while so all Patti had to do for a lot of it was to go back into their files although some of it was actually easier to just get on the information highway via her computer or to use her telephone. In fact, if Techno-Systems hadn't already been incorporated, the internet could have provided the most effective way to approach that. The state level of government was as accommodating as the federal government in most aspects of the services they each provided. Nowadays, for instance, an individual could form an LLC online themselves for a little over a hundred bucks initially and maintain it, again online, for about twenty-five bucks a year, depending on the state. Why "lawyer up" for everything before at least doing a simple search over the internet? A person can save a lot of time and money by jumping on the information highway.

Patti had actually noted a couple of items on her checklist that weren't mandatory for CCR registration but she wanted to cover all the bases. She really didn't believe the government would take note of the NAICS, SIC, PSC or FSC codes she researched and submitted on her registration form let alone call her if they needed anything. For one thing she wasn't sure of what all those damn initials stood for. The other thing was the unlikely thought of the government needing a specific item so they would call Techno-Systems out of all the companies listed. Still, you never know.

Some of the more salient points regarding Patti's earlier abbreviated check list included:

1. The DUNS (Data Universal Number System) number was free from Dun & Bradstreet by clicking on the link at the CCR website.

2. The TIN (Tax Identification Number) number was free from the IRS, or in the case of an individual sole proprietorship, a Social Security Number.

3. The nine digit zip code number was available from the post office.

4. The mm/dd/yyyy the business was formed or established.

5. The date the business (fiscal) year is closed for tax purposes.

6. Contact the Small Business Administration to find out if you're qualified for special consideration. Bill still hadn't met with the SBA specialist yet.

7. The NAICS (North American Industry Classification System) code numbers were free by referring to the CCR Handbook at the CCR website. While only one number was mandatory, up to twenty could be entered. Usually, the more the better.

8. The SIC (Standard Industrial Classification) numbers were ditto with the NAICS.

9. The PSC (Product Service Codes), also available in the handbook, were *not* mandatory. They applied to services and up to ten could be entered if so inclined. Ditto for the FSC (Federal Supply Classification) codes which applied to products.

10. The financial information was best supplied by the bank where Techno-Systems had their accounts. The ABA (American Banking Association) routing number turned out to be the first nine digits of the account number. The Automated Clearing House information was needed in case the government had problems with EFT (Electronic Funds Transfer) when they were trying to pay you. Getting paid was the best part of doing business with the government.

Patti had used the telephone to compile a couple of items on her list before completing the CCR registration form but could have done it all over the internet. She completed it in less than a half hour even though she had to interrupt herself twice, both times to get more data. Not too bad, she thought. It's my first day, I'm getting things done and I have a week-end ahead of me. She felt good.

Patti feeling good made Bill feel even better because he had a major crush on her. Ironically, Bill's first exposure to Patti was when Patti exposed herself to him. Oh, it was not like anything bad that Patti might have done, it was more Bill's perception of what he saw when he observed her in a bikini swimsuit. It was at a company picnic during the first sum-mer Bill worked at Techno-Systems, held at Patti and Denny's backyard swimming pool. What ever else Denny might have been, he was very good at making barbeque pork ribs. While Bill's eyes were often drawn in Patti's direction, she, along with more than a few others, were keeping their eyes on Jon, a buff looking guy in a Speedo.

Patti was not conscious of her effect on Bill, or probably the same effect she must have had on any other man that could breathe who saw her, looking so good and being totally unaware of it. Bill was still married then but Patti exuded sex appeal in Bill's mind and all she had to do was stand just right. When she did that, Bill could see a wider than he had ever seen, space between her extreme upper thighs. For some reason it was the most appealing thing Bill could ever remember seeing. Perhaps it was some deep down primal reaction to the perception of child bearing or some message to his libido of how accommodating she may be physically but, whatever, it sure pushed Bill's buttons.

After the picnic, every time Bill saw Patti at Techno-Systems, his eyes automatically dropped down, though almost always from her back. Bill didn't know if anyone else ever noticed his fixation but if Patti ever caught him staring while she might be facing him, he'd probably want to die on the spot. It was more weird than sick although Bill supposed that pretty much everybody in the world, including women, had some sort of a turn-on they kept to themselves. Bill wanted to be subtle for the sake of general office professionalism which was high on his list of ways to success.

The fixation never totally went away over the years though it either lightened enough or Bill was able to control it to a livable level. He didn't believe it was a case of Patti's body maturing past his obsessions because Bill had kept a pretty close watch on that aspect of her life. He did think her face had matured to be more beautiful than pretty but he of course kept that to himself.

4

Quality Assurance

First thing Monday morning Patti knocked on Bill's door. "Yes?" Bill said and softened when Patti said, "Just me."

Patti opened the door and peeked her head in. "We're officially on our way. We'll get verification in a day or so but for now I'm ready for the next project, boss."

The "boss" part made Bill a little uncomfortable because Patti used to sit at the desk he was occupying at the present.

"Come in. Please, sit down, Patti." Patti did. "I suppose we have to look at our quality assurance to see if it's okay for the feds," Bill said, "I'll see if Kevin is available." Kevin was in charge of their inspection department and had been for almost five years. "Just to be a little more professional, I'm going to change Kevin's job title to 'Quality Assurance Manager' and offer him a little bump in pay." Patti nodded her head. Part of Bill's plan to grow the company was to make everyone in key jobs feel more professional by upgrading their titles and delegating more responsibilities.

In that spirit, Bill had gone to the local library one night and checked-out a book on management. The book suggested writing fairly comprehensive job descriptions for a few key positions and getting those persons to buy into them. Their agreeing to the position's stated requirements and both parties signing the paper was a big step towards a clear understanding of what was expected. The employee had a sense of ownership and Bill had another piece of his plan firmed-up.

Kevin was Jeremy's younger brother and had started well after Jeremy had been a machine operator for awhile. Jeremy and Kevin moved up in their respective departments based on good old-fashioned hard work and by being dependable employees. Bill wasn't sure about having both brothers in management positions because as the Production Supervisor, Jeremy could easily be at odds with inspection but they both assured Bill that it would work. And so far, it had worked great. Where Kevin was in his late forties, tall and dark complexioned, Jeremy had recently turned fifty, shorter, also dark complexioned but with a slightly pitted face and heavy lidded eyes, like he was always tired.

"Hi Kevin. When you get a minute can you come to the office?" said Bill as soon as Kevin answered his page. "Sure Bill. Be right there." Then Kevin added that he'd bring his notes on what he'd researched regarding the federal governments requirements.

"Hi Patti," said Kevin when he got to Bill's office. "Hi Kevin," replied Patti. Kevin had had a few disagreements with Patti around the same time as Jeremy when she was trying to force everything through production. At the time, she accused Kevin of being a lot fussier then than when he was the inspector for her ex. Though Kevin, unlike Jeremy, would show his emotions by getting outwardly mad right away and then forgetting it later.

"So, what do you have?" queried Bill. Kevin had gotten a heads-up a couple of months ago on his future mission and made the best of it by searching the internet. There was a glut of information to pass on to Bill and Patti but Kevin diplomatically asked if he could first review the theory and basics of quality and its resulting systems. The review was really in deference to Patti's lack of manufacturing knowledge.

Kevin began by what quality was. Simply put, quality is what the customer says it is or conformance to stated requirements. Quality has a characteristic in that it can be measured in both products and services. If all the measurements add up to what the customer defined or needed, then what you have just provided is quality. If something cannot be measured, in theory it cannot possess quality.

Every customer wants a quality product or service and the government is probably more demanding than most. They use a predetermined concept of form, fit and function in their expectation of quality but without the flexibility of some end users. When the government purchases products or services from a company, the company is held to a much defined standard of quality as specified in the contract. The level of quality standard that the company is required to meet depends on the product or service being purchased.

An old manufacturing adage suggests that "if you can measure something in your shop, you can probably make it." This is in reference to the close link between manufacturing a part and the subsequent inspection of that part to prove its quality. Both go hand and hand and both evolve at the same rate of whatever product that shop produces. The link between a service provided and measurement of that service is usually not quite as clear as a specific product even though it is just as important.

The point being, the Quality System for a company seeking to be a supplier to the United States Federal Government must be at least adequate to assure the product or service meets the stated requirements. The range of tools and systems necessary could be a simple tape measure, provided by the vendor and checked annually, to complex electronic devices and standards provided by the government.

Nowadays, quality is a given throughout every industry. The entire government and all commercial customers expect quality from every supplier. If a supplier does not provide a quality product or service, they cannot compete and will most likely go out of business, or at least will not do business with the government for very long. A supplier's performance history is paramount to doing repeat business with the government.

A Quality System is the overall program; Quality Assurance proves the product or service meets expected specifications and Quality Control is used in the manufacturing of a product or the rendering of a service. Both assurance and control are necessary if the supplier expects the government to accept the product or service and, most important to the well-being of the supplier, the supplier makes an adequate profit. When a supplier is committed to a contract, it is their responsibility to furnish an acceptable product or service regardless of the cost.

Of course the government would prefer to see the supplier be profitable although their first concern is to have their contract fulfilled. Ultimately it is up to the vendor to plan, quote, produce, deliver to specifications and still make a profit. If the vendor has an effective Quality System in place they minimize the risk of unplanned problems cutting into their profits.

Extra material costs may be somewhat negotiable with the government if addressed in advance but mistakes due to an ineffective Quality System will elicit no sympathy from Uncle Sam.

Again, selling to the government is not a lot different from selling to commercial accounts from the standpoint of quality. Any company supplying a quality product or service to commercial accounts shouldn't have any problems supplying quality to the government. Always planning hard for success usually produces success.

The federal government utilizes different levels and types of quality as necessary for the complexity of the product or service being provided. As usual, a quick search on the internet will produce the most current requirements for general types of contracts while the specific requirements are found on the bid and/or the contract.

Before Kevin went any further, he asked if it would be okay to take a break. Bill looked at Patti and she wriggled her eyebrows a couple of times so a break was called. Kevin had to check on project going through the shop besides having nature calling.

Twenty minutes later, Bill, Patti and Kevin were back in Bill's office. Kevin passed out copies of part of Part 46 of the Federal Acquisition Regulation (FAR) pertaining to the four basic Quality Assurance Systems used by the federal government. He had been reading official government information for the last week and wanted to give Patti and Bill a feel for it.

The printed copies looked like this:

46.202 Types of contract quality requirements.

Contract quality requirements fall into four general categories, depending on the extent of quality assurance needed by the Government for acquisition involved.

46.202-1 Contracts for commercial items.

When acquiring commercial items (see Part 12), the Government shall rely on contractors' existing quality assurance systems as a substitute for Government inspection and testing before tender for acceptance unless customary market practices for the commercial item being acquired include in-process inspection. Any in-process inspection by the Government shall be conducted in a manner consistent with commercial practice.

46.202-2 Government reliance on inspection by contractor.
(a) Except as specified in (b) of this section, the Government shall rely on the contractor to accomplish all inspection and testing needed to ensure that supplies or services acquired at or below the simplified acquisition threshold conform to contract quality requirements before they are tendered to the Government (see 46.301).

(b) The Government shall not rely on inspection by the contractor if the contracting officer determines that the Government has a need to test the supplies or services in advance of their tender for acceptance, or to pass judgment upon the adequacy of the contractor's internal work processes. In making the determination, the contracting officer shall consider—

(1) The nature of the supplies and services being purchased and their intended use:

(2) The potential losses in the event of defects;

(3) The likelihood of uncontested replacement or correction of defective work; and

(4) The cost of detailed Government inspection.

46.202-3 Standard inspection requirements.
(a) Standard inspection requirements are contained in the clauses prescribed in 46.302 through 46.308, and 46.310, and in the product and service specifications that are included in solicitations and contracts.

(b) The clauses referred to in (a) of this section-

(1) Require the contractor to provide and maintain an inspection system that is acceptable to the Government;

(2) Give the Government the right to make inspections and tests while work is in process; and

(3) Require the contractor to keep complete, and make available to the Government, records of its inspection work.

46-202-4 Higher-level contract quality requirements.

(a) Requiring compliance with higher-level quality standards is appropriate in solicitations and contracts for complex or critical items (see 46.203(b) or ©) or when the technical requirements of the contract require-

(b) When the contracting officer, in consultation with technical personnel, finds it is in the Government's interest to require that higher-level quality standards be maintained, the contracting officer shall use the clause prescribed at 46.311. The contracting officer shall indicate in the clause which higher-level quality standards will satisfy the Government's requirement. Examples of higher-level quality standards are ISO 9001, 9002, or 9003; ANSI/ISO/ASQ Q9001-2000; ANSI/ASQC Q9001, Q9002, or Q9003; QS-9000; AZ-9000; AMSO/ASQC E4; and ANSI/ASME NQA-1.

"If the contract dollar amount is over $100,000, standard inspection requirements usually apply, like 46.202-3, unless the non-commercial item is critical or the complexity requires a higher level quality program" Kevin went on to explain. "Bill, you mentioned doing work for a prime contractor as a subcontractor to avoid the government stuff. But the government's requirements may trickle down at the prime's discretion."

"Who's liable if there's a problem?" asked Bill. Kevin offered "I suppose if the prime picked the subcontractor to do work, the prime is responsible in the end. Subcontracting is very competitive and the primes call the shots. Too many problems and the prime may find another subcontractor. Here's a copy of a FAR requirement for subcontractors."

Kevin handed each of them another copy:

46.405 Subcontracts.

(a) Government contract quality assurance on subcontracted supplies or services shall be performed only when required in the Government's interest. The primary purpose is to assist the contract administration office cognizant of the prime contractor's plant in determining the conformance of subcontracted supplies or services with contract requirements or to satisfy one or more of the factors included in (b) of this section. It does not relieve the prime contractor of any responsibilities under the contract. When appropriate, the prime contractor shall be requested to arrange for timely Government access to the subcontractor facility.

(b) The Government shall perform quality assurance at the subcontract level when-

(1) The item is to be shipped from the subcontractor's plant to the using activity and inspection at source is required;

(2) The conditions for quality assurance at source are applicable (see 46.402);

(3) The contract specifies that certain quality assurance functions, which can be performed only at the subcontractor's plant, are to be performed by the Government; or

(4) It is otherwise required by the contract or determined to be in the Government's interest.

(c) Supplies or services for which certificates, records, reports, or similar evidence of quality are available at the prime contractor's plant shall not be inspected at the subcontractor's plant, except occasionally to verify this evidence or when required under (b) of this section.

(d) All oral and written statements and contract terms and conditions relating to Government quality assurance actions at the subcontract level shall be worded so as not to-

(1) Affect the contractual relationship between the prime contractor and the Government, or between the prime contractor and the subcontractor;

(2) Establish a contractual relationship between the Government and the subcontractor; or

(3) Constitute a waiver of the Government's right to accept or reject the supplies or services.

Patti, looking at the Federal Acquisition Regulation copies, shook her head. "Do we have to read all of this legal mumbo jumbo for everything?" she asked Kevin then added "it makes me feel a little dumb. I'm not, but I'm not a lawyer."

"I don't really think we'll be referring to the 'FAR' too often, if ever, but we should be a little familiar with it and how to find it. When I visited their website, the regulation book was huge and I doubt that many lawyers would know much about it," replied Kevin. "Like most engineers, they probably just know where to look."

"Another interesting point is the Mil-Spec 45208 Bill was always telling me about has been replaced by ISO standards, but I understand some of the buyers who've been around a while still refer to it." Kevin continued to elaborate on a few outdated specs that were apparently still near and dear to some in the system.

MIL-STD-45662 was in reference to inspection equipment. It explained the how, why and what a company did to establish and maintain a system of all the measurement and test equipment used in the contract. Kevin added that it was replaced by an ISO Calibration Systems Requirements ISO 10012-1, ANSI/NCSL Z540-1.

MIL-I-45208, Bill's oft mentioned spec, was entitled "An Inspection System." This quality pertained to military items and set forth the objectives and essential elements of an inspection system. It was referenced in a contract whenever an inspection system was required for an item, probably why Bill heard it so much. This system was used when technical requirements required in-process as well as final end item inspection, including control of measuring and testing equipment, drawings and changes, documentation and records. It impacted both large and small businesses alike. Basically, it meant that a company had to document its inspection system to assure continuity.

MIL-Q-9858A was entitled "A Quality Program" and was used whenever the contract involved complex types of military hardware and systems. It may still be referenced when the technical requirements of a contract require control of work operations, in-process control, inspection, organization, work instructions, documentation control and advanced metrology although ISO addresses those issues as well.

Kevin also covered the "Certificate of Conformance" that could be provided for in the contract if product history was excellent. It's used at the discretion of the contracting officer instead of source inspection for the convenience of the government, not the supplier.

Bill interrupted Kevin, "Could you tell Patti about ISO? That's the direction I want to go." Kevin said, "sure," and went on with his presentation.

Kevin explained that ISO stood for the "International Organization for Standards" though he had read that it was probably from the Greek word *isos* meaning equal. Right after WWII, the problems of different standards from different countries was discussed. The problem was each country not only having their own standards for quality, they disagreed what quality really was. In 1947, international standards for quality were developed in Geneva, Switzerland. Now, the ISO organization comprises a worldwide federation of over 100 countries. The goal is to make everyone equal.

In Europe, registration to the ISO standard has become virtually a prerequisite for doing business. In the United States, almost all of the larger companies recognize ISO registered suppliers as having an effective Quality System and would usually prefer to do business with them. For example, if you want to be a supplier to America's largest automakers, you have to be registered to QS-9000, a quality system model which embraces the precepts of ISO 9000 in its entirety.

Other large companies, when considering a new supplier, usually have a lengthy question form regarding a potential suppliers quality practices to judge their quality system. If a supplier has been registered to the ISO Quality Standards, they enter their registration number on the first page of the form and are able to skip the rest. That supplier has already proven their quality system is acceptable. Kevin then added it didn't necessarily guarantee the specific quality of a particular item but they at least had the means to catch errors and that in itself was assuring.

The ISO system was set-up to encourage continuous improvement by the registered company. Kevin ticked-off a few other benefits:

- International recognition

- Proven Quality System

- Defects prevented

- Productivity increased

- Costs reduced

- Waste reduced

- Access to a global marketplace

- Access to the government marketplace was easier

Being an ISO registered company set them apart from other companies and would have to help them for subcontracting, Kevin added. Techno-Systems was not ISO registered but Kevin went on to explain how he was formatting their quality program to the ISO 9000 standards so if and when they pursued registration, it would already be partially done.

Then came the most compelling reason to base their quality program on the ISO standards. "It's possible the government may require all of their suppliers to be ISO certified someday," said Kevin. "If we're serious about this government business, we have to plan ahead. The government uses different filters to reduce the number of responding suppliers to save their personal time as much as anything. I can do it, Bill."

"I'm not worried about your ability, Kevin. I know you can do it. What do you think Patti? You know. This whole ISO thing," asked Bill.

"What the inspection department does doesn't affect me. I'm just helping you out in the office and with this government thing," replied Patti, "but I'm in your hands, boss." She was flirting a little. Still, Bill didn't like anyone calling him boss because a long time ago, he was told that a "boss" was a double S.O.B. spelled backwards. Another person had told him "if you're the boss and I'm nothing, that makes you the boss of nothing."

Instead of saying anything about not being a boss, Bill said, "From what I understand about ISO, it's not just the inspection department, it's pretty much the whole company getting involved to be ISO certified."

Kevin nodded, "I spoke to a guy who's been through an ISO registration and he said it's important to get everyone to 'buy in' if we hope to do it in a reasonable amount of time. I've heard it can take anywhere from six months to two years. It'll be easier if everybody wants it to work."

Bill didn't say anything else. He was thinking about Patti's comment of being in his hands.

All of a sudden, Bill's mind came back. He looked like he just remembred an important point. "Tell Patti about the credit card thing and ISO." Kevin went on to explain that ISO standards contain provisions for precise criteria for the features and characteristics of products and services to assure their universal acceptance. For example, the format of credit cards is derived from an ISO international standard, which defines such features as the optimal thickness (0.76 mm) of each card so that all the cards could be used worldwide on the same reading equipment.

The scope of ISO covers all technical fields, except electrical and electronic engineering, which is the responsibility of the International Electrotechnical Commission (IEC). The IEC is the international standards and conformity assessment body for all fields of electro-technology.

Kevin had the feeling he may be losing his audience pretty soon so he decided to wrap-up his presentation. He told them the ISO 9001.2000 Quality Management System was comprehensive and was organized in the same order as you would normally do something; that is to say it's a process approach. A process is a series of steps or actions that do something in a logical sequence. Example:

1. First you would plan it.

2. Then you would do it.

3. Then you would check and analyze what you did.

4. Lastly, You would improve on how you did it.

Kevin briefly mentioned ISO 14000, the environmental version of ISO 9000. It ensures control over environmental aspects of services, products and activities and the impacts they cause. Users include companies like Ford Motor Co., Texas Instruments and Bristol-Myers. Kevin was about to discuss specifically what his plan was to implement a very ISO-like program when he was interrupted.

"Mr. Nelson?" like a question. It was the receptionist, sticking her head in Bill's office door. "There's someone here to see you. They were asking about Patti, uh, Mrs. Bell, and said they'd like to talk to you too."

"Sure, send them in" Bill answered. "Kevin, could you excuse us?"

"Hi, I'm Bill Nelson and this is Patti Bell" Bill said to the woman who had materialized beside Mary. Then Bill also noticed a man right behind Mary and said hello to him, then "Please, come in."

"I'm Detective Barbara Phelps, this is Detective Craig Meadows" announced the woman. Detective Meadows just nodded and moved in beside her. "Mrs. Bell, your neighbor said you would probably be here. Is there a place we could talk in private?"

Patti was obviously nervous. "Bill, could we use the conference room? Or maybe, I don't mind talking in front of Bill. If that's okay, I mean." to Detective Phelps who looked at Bill.

"Sure, That's fine with me" acknowledged Bill "Please have a seat" then moved over to the door and closed it.

Detective Phelps must have been in charge because the other detective seemed to defer to her. "Mrs. Bell, we're from Homicide. We regret to inform you that your ex-husband, Dennis Bell, was found dead this morning at his company."

5

ISO 9001:2000

Patti started to standup, sat back down and put her hands to the sides of her face. She was absolutely speechless. Bill just looked confused.

Detectives Phelps and Meadows were watching both Patti and Bill to see their initial reaction. Then Detective Phelps spoke, "Mr. Bell was found in the shop area of his company. He was obviously murdered."

The detective didn't want to give any details immediately of how Dennis must have died. It was not only bizarre, it was horrific. At first glance, it didn't look bad other than the usual distress of looking a dead person, until you studied the scene.

Dennis was discovered at 6:45 a.m., that Monday, when his employees started rolling in for the day. Joe, his foreman, had turned on the lights and was walking by the water jet machine. He yelled "whoa" when he saw a person laying on the worktable, then figured out it was his boss, and he had turned white as a ghost, just a shade paler than Joe right then.

The water jet was a machine capable of cutting up to 8 inches thick steel with a stream of water and abrasive at 60,000 psi, directed over the work piece by a computer control. The kerf, or the width of the finished cut was only about 1/32nd of an inch or .033 and produced neat, smooth edges. The table of the machine was large and looked like the kind of steel grating found on mezzanines.

Dennis must have been tied to the grating when he was unconscious or incapacitated in some way because it didn't appear that he put up much resistance. In fact, his expression was peaceful, like he was having a nice nap. There were blood stains on his inner right thigh and to the right of his groin, less and less blood up to his waist then nothing but a line straight up and through the right side of his face. Other than Dennis' unworldly pasty color, he could have been sleeping.

The horror part was when the ME touched the head and it fell in half. Dennis had been neatly bisected by the water jet. He had bled out into the machine's water reservoir which accounted for his white coloring. The sight reminded one of the responding policeman of a side of beef in a meat processing plant. Ironically, the ME had to tie him together like a rolled roast before they could move him.

Mercifully, if Dennis wasn't dead, he must have been unconscious when it happened or the scene would have obviously been violent.

"My God," exclaimed Bill without even knowing the sordid details. Patti was still speechless with her hands to her face.

The detectives weren't totally sure what to expect of Patti and Bill's reactions. They both seemed genuinely surprised over the dropped bomb and Patti closed her eyes and opened her mouth while Bill seemed to be thinking hard, sorting it out. The detectives would separate them before asking too many details but Bill offered that he hadn't seen Dennis for months. Neither detective acknowledged even hearing Bill, instead looking at each other, like something was passing between them.

"Mrs. Bell. Could you please come down to the station with us?" this from Phelps.

"Surely you don't suspect Patti," said Bill. Patti opened her eyes and looked at Bill.

The other detective flashed a semi-irritated glance at Bill too, as if to caution him.

Phelps didn't answer though she did offer, "We'll be talking to both of you today just like we'll be talking to a lot of people. It's how we conduct an investigation. We ask lots of questions and often take statements from the people closest to the deceased."

Bill said, "Patti, should I call my lawyer? You know him, Eric Fredrickson."

"I've got Jane, she took care of the divorce," Patti replied.

"Please, please, calm down. This is just standard procedure. Mrs. Bell, you can ride with Detective Meadows and me. Another team will be here in a few minutes to talk to you, Mr. Nelson."

"Sure. I understand this is routine. I'm just at a loss right now."

Bill shook the detectives' hands and had an immediate bad feeling about the guy, Meadows, simply based on his poor handshaking technique. In a good handshake, both parties held out their hands with the thumb and fingers forming a wide "V" towards each other, both parties being patient until their hands made contact before firmly grasping. Detective Meadows grabbed Bill's fingertips too early, squeezing too hard, making Bill think that he was inexperienced or impetuous or something not good.

Patti and Bill were both questioned, Patti for well over two-hours, Bill only for about fifty-minutes. Later that afternoon, they met back at Techno-Systems. Bill had work to take care of right away and Patti didn't know where else to go. She wasn't planning on being involved with funeral arrangements and besides, she still had to collect her thoughts. She and Dennis had severed most of their ties with the divorce but there had to be something she'd have to do. Too soon. Too complicated. Were there any ramifications? There was too much to think about all at once.

"Patti?" Bill noticed her staring off somewhere. "How did your interview go?"

"Gosh, well it didn't feel like an interrogation, but they wanted to check out a few things and talk to me later."

"I was cleared for now too. Yesterday, I had the girls all day until maybe 9 o'clock last night." The girls were Becky and Britney, ages ten and thirteen, from his defunct marriage. Bill had been divorced for almost seven years and still didn't have much of a social life other than the kids every other weekend, and work. He added, "they figured Denny was murdered mid to late afternoon, but weren't sure yet because of the weird circumstances."

"Weird is way too mild. When I first heard the details wasn't as bad as after I thought about it. Good grief!"

"I know what you mean, Patti. If anything changes, they said they'd get back to me. I spent last night at home, doing nothing. I suppose I could be a suspect but the cops weren't really too interested in me. I think."

"I suppose I could be a suspect too. Mostly because they said the spouse usually is. They asked me if I knew how to run the water jet and I told them no. One of Denny's machinists told them it didn't take much to make the machine do something so simple, but I told them 'I know *nothing* about how' they seemed to believe me," said Patti.

"Denny must've had eighty pounds on you, especially dead weight, oops."

"That's okay. Actually, Bill, the latest theory was that he was alive when the machine started working, but, yes, he had to be totally out of it."

"Well, let me know if I can do anything for you."

"Sure, you're sweet. I could have used an alibi if you could've helped me with that. I spent yesterday and last night alone, as usual."

Bill gave that scenario a little thought and they spoke for a few more minutes and called it a day. Patti left right away while Bill stayed another hour before leaving.

Over two days had passed without much more incident. Dennis' time of death had been put at between 4 and 5 o'clock on Sunday afternoon, officially clearing Bill for now. Patti had been questioned twice more and still didn't seem to be of major interest to the police. In fact, all the police had gathered during that period was that Dennis Bell had not been very well-liked. His business ethics were questionable and his reputation was certainly tarnished, unless you were a good-paying customer that is. Dennis Bell gave great world-class customer service.

Bill organized another meeting with Kevin and Patti to finish-up their quality issues. It would be right after lunch on this afternoon, Thursday. Kevin had put together a rough draft of a potential Quality Manual. Patti's next assignment was to start prospecting for government business. Tomorrow, Bill had an appointment with the SBA representative, who requested a plant tour. Everything was sort of getting back to normal except for a possible new opportunity.

Dennis' new company, Systems-Plus, was not and could not be opened for business until the smoke cleared, whenever that might be. The employees had all already filed for unemployment benefits to carry them for awhile but what would happen in the long term to the state of the art company?

It appeared so far no one was either available or interested in taking over the company. Dennis had not had any relatives with manufacturing experience or inclination. Besides, the business was new with a ton of start-up debt and the customers were there because of Dennis, not the company itself. Most of the customers would probably revert back to Techno-Systems, particularly since they originally came from there anyway.

Bill was secretly entertaining the thought of trying to buy Systems-Plus and merging it with his company. He'd be counting on getting it for pennies on the dollar for the whole shebang. A couple of its employees, Bill's ex-employees, had already expressed interest in coming back to Techno-Systems. Only one of the people who had left, a guy with an infamously poor attitude problem, had "burned their bridges."

Bill wouldn't take Donny back even if he had left under better circumstances. He was a proficient enough worker but he brought down everybody around him over the damnedest things. Every one was glad to see him go at Techno-Systems but the others at Systems-Plus were not happy to see him coming on board, except Dennis, because Donny was a suck-up. He was the kind of person who nobody said hello when he came into a room, but who everybody said goodbye to when he left.

He was the only one that had left who Bill was glad to see go because it made a decision easy for him. Bill had grown terminally tired of Donny's disruptive antics. Donny had an infectious personality but was usually mad at society or anyone else who didn't think like him, unfortunately the rest of society. If he walked up to you and you were in a good mood but he wasn't, you'd better change right now.

Bill didn't mind getting rid of somebody if he knew, deep down inside, it was not for a personal reason. He had learned long ago that it was better to go through a little agony once during a dismissal than to go through everyday with a sour employee. And, who knows, maybe the employee would be happier someplace else, although that wouldn't be Bill's primary concern. Bill actually *owed* it to the remaining employees for it was his responsibility to provide a healthy place for them to work.

After lunch, the three of them met back in Bill's office to hear the rest of Kevin's presentation. Kevin had been a busy man. "Kevin, you've been a busy boy," said Patti. He started by handing Patti and Bill each a copy of the Quality Manual he had cobbled together in record time.

"How did you do this so fast?" asked Bill.

"I'll explain it later," said Kevin. "It's just a rough draft but the essence of it probably won't change much. I based the format and the content on the ISO 9001:2000 model. I really like the ISO concepts, and the more I learn about them, the more I like."

Kevin went on to relate to them why and how this came to be. He had ordered a hard copy of the ISO 9001:2000 Standards from the American Society for Quality, or ASQ, before a friend, a fellow inspector from another manufacturer, offered to let them use his copy of the standards until the new one arrived. His friend also allowed Kevin to see their Quality Manual to use as a guide but told him not to copy anything word for word. He said it was not only wrong, it wasn't effective. All of the ISO 9001:2000 registered firms had Quality Manuals based on exactly the same set of published standards, although each company had customized their particular manual. Every step taken in the ISO registration process would be customized even more.

The four major steps or elements of an ISO program were:

1. The published Standards.

2. Quality Manual—customized.

3. Procedures—customized more "what to do" instructions.

4. Work Instructions—customized, detailed even more "how to do" instructions.

Kevin had heard of a company combining the procedures and work instructions although he hadn't delved deep enough to know what was fact and what was fiction. For Techno-Systems purposes at this point, combining them would save time.

Kevin explained that if they went with the ISO content as a basis for their Quality System, and pursued a formal registration later, the procedures and the work instructions could be reformatted if necessary. He then proceeded to go through the rough draft manual, covering each section:

(cover page)

Techno-Systems, Inc.

Quality Assurance Manual

Approved:

_____

William P. Nelson—President

_____

Kevin Johnson—Quality Mgr.

(next page)

Quality Manual: Table of contents

Number Section		**Page Number**
1.	**General**	
1.1.	Revision status	
1.2.	Purpose and scope	
1.3.	Exclusions	
2.	**Company background and history**	
3.	**Definitions and abbreviations**	
4.	**Quality Management system**	
4.1.	General requirements	
4.2.	Documentation requirements	

(first page)

1.   General

1.1.   Revision status and history

Rev/Description of change   **Date/Approved**

(next page)

1.1. Purpose and scope

This Quality Manual documents our quality system in order to demonstrate Techno-Systems, Inc.'s ability to consistently provide products that meet or exceed customer and regulatory requirements.

The format and numbering of this Quality Manual directly corresponds to the format and numbering of ISO 9001:2000. Although we are not formally certified, we strive to comply with the standards as set forth in ISO 9001:2000. This policy is encouraged throughout the entire process with the intention of eventual certification as necessary.

1.3. Exclusions

Where any requirement of ISO 9001:2000 can not be applied due to the nature of our organization, it will be considered for exclusion. The exclusion will not affect our ability, nor absolves us from the responsibility, to provide product that meets customer and applicable regulatory requirements.

The Quality Assurance Manager is responsible for identifying those requirements that do not apply to our organization and to propose exclusions of such requirements from the scope of our quality system.

The President of the company has the responsibility and authority for examining whether the proposed exclusions are appropriate and for approving them. Evaluation and approval of possible exclusions are conducted within the framework of management reviews of the quality system.

If an exclusion is approved, it will be documented and all concerned will be made aware of the situation.

Again, it is our sincere desire to comply with all precepts within the scope of ISO 9001:2000 when practical or possible.

(next page)

2. Company background and history

(next page)

3. Definitions and abbreviations

Corrective action—Action taken after a non-conforming event has occurred.

Customer Property—Articles provided by the customer where the customer retains ownership. Articles may be part of the finished product, used for inspection purposes or to custom fit to a customer component.

Design—This applies to new product.

Exclusion—A process of the QMS possibly not implemented at this point in time, although it may be a goal to implement it in the future as resources permit.

Management review—Interested parties meeting to discuss the QMS status at prescribed intervals.

Measurement of QMS—Using data such as statistical information or benchmarking values.

Non-Conforming—Does not meet specifications and/or requirements.

Preventive action—Action taken before a non-conforming event occurs.

Product realization—This is the same as product manufacturing as used in this Quality Manual.

QMS—Quality Management System.

QMT—Quality Management Team.

(next pages)

4. Quality management system

4.1. General requirements

Techno-Systems, Inc. has established, documented, implemented and maintains a Quality Management System and continually improves its effectiveness.

Techno-Systems, Inc.'s Quality Management System:

- identifies the processes needed for its operations and their application throughout the organization.

- determines the sequence and interaction of these primary processes.

- determines criteria and methods needed to ensure that both the operation and management of these processes are effective.

- ensures the availability of resources and information necessary to support the operation and monitoring of these resources.

- ensures monitoring, measurement and analysis of these processes.

- ensures implementation of actions necessary to achieve planned results and continual improvement of these processes.

Where any processes that affect product conformity with requirements are outsourced, the company ensures management of such processes.

4.2. Documentation requirements

Quality Management System documentation includes the quality policy, quality objectives, a quality manual, documented records and other documents necessary to ensure effective planning, operation and control.

Document control is an ongoing process and includes:

- initial approval, issue, review, revision and re-approval of documents.

- identification of changes and the current revision status of documents.

- ensuring that relevant versions of applicable documents are available at points of use.

- ensuring that documents remain legible and readily identifiable.

- ensuring that documents of external origin are identified and their distribution is controlled.

- prevention of unintended use of obsolete documents.

5. Management responsibility

5.1. Management responsibility

Techno-Systems, Inc. provides evidence of its commitment to the development, implementation and continual improvement of the QMS by:

- communicating to the organization the importance of meeting customer requirements.

- establishing the quality policy.

- ensuring quality objectives are established and met.

- conducting management reviews.

- ensuring the availability of necessary resources.

5.2. Customer focus

Techno-Systems, Inc.'s management ensures that all customer requirements are determined and fulfilled.

Our goal is total customer satisfaction … Techno-Systems, Inc. is committed to providing customers with products that meet or exceed customer expectations.

5.3 Quality policy

Techno-Systems, Inc. has adopted the following Quality Policy:

?

5.4. Quality system planning

Techno-Systems, Inc.'s management ensures that quality objectives are established at all levels within the organization. The quality objectives are measurable and consistent with the quality policy.

The company management ensures that planning of the QMS is carried out in order to meet the requirements found in **4.1** of this manual and that the integrity of the QMS is maintained when changes are planned and implemented.

5.5. Organization and communication

Techno-Systems, Inc.'s management ensures that responsibilities, authorities and their interrelation are defined and communicated with all concerned.

5.6. Management review

Techno-Systems, Inc.'s management reviews the QMS at least annually to ensure its continuing suitability, adequacy and effectiveness while assessing opportunities for improvement.

Inputs to management review include information on:

- results of audits.
- customer feedback.
- process performance and conformance.
- status of preventive and corrective actions.
- follow-up actions from previous management reviews.

- planned changes that could affect the QMS.
- recommendations for improvement.

The outputs from the management review include decisions and actions related to:

- improvement of the QMS and its processes.
- improvement of service related to customer requirements.
- resource needs.

6. Resource management

6.1. Provision of resources

Techno-Systems, Inc. determines and provides the resources needed to implement and maintain the QMS and continually improves its effectiveness in enhancing customer satisfaction by meeting customer requirements.

6.2. Human resources and training

Techno-Systems, Inc. ensures that personnel performing work affecting quality are competent on the basis of training and skills.

Employees are indoctrinated and trained, as necessary, to ensure that suitable proficiency is achieved and maintained throughout our operating systems. Some training is performed as "On the Job Training" under the direct supervision of management. Procedural changes are implemented by training of any individual(s) affected by the change.

All employees are aware of the relevance and importance of their activities and how they contribute to the achievement of the quality objectives.

6.3. Infrastructure and work environment

Techno-Systems, Inc. determines, provides and maintains the infrastructure needed to achieve conformity to customer and quality requirements.

Techno-Systems, Inc. determines the work environment needed to achieve conformity to customer and quality requirements.

7. Product realization

7.1. Planning of product realization

Techno-Systems, Inc. plans and develops the processes needed for product realization. Planning of product realization is consistent with the QMS.

In planning product realization, we determine, as appropriate, the following:

- quality objectives and requirements for the product.
- the need to establish processes, documents, and provide resources specific to the product.
- required verification, validation monitoring, inspection and test activities specific to the product.
- the criteria for customer acceptance of the product.
- records needed to provide the evidence that the realization process and the resulting product fulfill requirements.

7.2. Customer related processes

Techno-Systems, Inc. determines:

- requirements specified by the customer.
- requirements not stated by the customer but specified or known for intended use.
- any additional requirements determined by Techno-Systems, Inc.

7.3. Design

On new products, Techno-Systems, Inc. works with the customer to determine the needs of the product and the customer. The customer clearly states their requirements either verbally or through written information. The customer accepts the design through a documented method, preferably a purchase order.

The customer is liable for the design after they have approved it.

7.4. Purchasing

Techno-Systems, Inc. ensures that purchased items and services conform to the customer's requirements and specifications as stated on their purchasing documents.

Techno-Systems, Inc. evaluates and selects suppliers and/or contractors based on their ability to supply and/or provide service consistent with our customer's requirements.

Criteria for selection may be based on our customer's specific requirements in regard to necessary certifications to ensure compliance. Certain inspection methods may "trickle down" to subcontractors to satisfy our customer's quality requirements.

7.5. Operations

Techno-Systems, Inc. ensures that processes are identified, applied and monitored to the satisfaction of the QMS.

7.5.1. Operations control

For each of the processes, we:

- provide acceptance criteria for a job well done.
- have work instructions, pictures or notes on how to perform that process or task.
- make sure the process and equipment are capable of what we want.
- monitor and adjust the critical parameters of the process.
- implement follow-through processes for release, delivery, technical service and after-sales service.

7.5.2. Identification and traceability

Techno-Systems, Inc. identifies the product by suitable means for each specific job being processed with respect to measurement and monitoring requirements

7.5.3. Customer property

Techno-Systems, Inc. exercises care with customer property while it is under our control, being used by us or incorporated into the product. If any customer property is lost, damaged or found to be unsuitable for use, it is reported to the customer and records maintained.

7.5.4. Preservation of product

Techno-Systems, Inc. preserves product integrity throughout internal processing and storage of components and the finished product.

7.6. Inspection, measurement and test equipment

Calibration is performed on equipment traceable to recognized national standards at prescribed intervals by qualified calibration services as necessary to maintain accuracy.

Calibration of commercial equipment (i.e. operator owned rulers, tape measures, calipers, micrometers, etc,) is monitored by management to ensure accuracy. Management reserves the right to request that any questionable equipment be removed from service.

Company owned equipment is identified with current status of calibration and records are maintained. Items too small to be identified by marking are serialized and calibration status is maintained by a traceable record supporting a calibration recall system.

Overall, the equipment necessary to ensure accurate data to the customer and to assure quality is maintained in good working condition.

Ref: Calibration Systems Requirements ISO 10012-1, ANSI/NCSL Z540-1

8. Measurement, analysis and improvement

8.1. Planning of monitoring and measuring

Techno-Systems, Inc. monitors information relating to customer satisfaction and internal audits to determine if there are any resource constraints, anticipated or unanticipated.

We plan the audit program, taking into consideration the status and priorities of the processes to be audited and the results of previous audits. The audit criteria, scope, frequency and methods are defined. Auditors do not audit their own work.

Management responsible for the area audited ensures actions are taken without undue delay to eliminate detected non-conformities and root causes. Follow-up activities include the verification of the action taken and the reporting of the verification results.

8.2. Monitoring and measurement

Techno-Systems, Inc. applies suitable methods for monitoring and, where applicable, measurement of the QMS processes. These methods ensure the ability of the process to achieve planned results. When planned results are not achieved, correction and corrective action are taken to ensure conformity to the proper requirements.

Product process and delivery do not proceed until new work plans have been satisfactorily completed or unless otherwise approved and documented by the customer.

8.3. Control of non-conforming product

All non-conforming product is clearly identified and kept well away from conforming product. A special area is designated for non-conforming articles and products.

All non-conforming articles and product are reviewed to determine disposition and decisions are documented on the accompanying paperwork.

The quality manager approves all dispositions of non-conforming articles to:

- return to supplier.
- rework to specification.
- scrap.

Customer approval of non-conforming articles or product must be documented.

8.4. Analysis of quality information

Techno-Systems, inc. determines, collects and analyzes appropriate data to demonstrate the suitability and effectiveness of the QMS and continual improvement can be made.

We analyze this data to provide information on:

- customer satisfaction.
- conformance to requirements.
- characteristics and trends of processes including opportunities for preventive actions.
- supplies.

8.5. Continual improvement

Techno-Systems, Inc. continually improves the effectiveness of the QMS through the use of the Quality Policy, quality objectives, audit data, corrective and preventive actions and the management review.

8.5.1. Planning for continual improvement

Techno-Systems, Inc. is continually planning improvement of their products and processes based on input from customers, employees, management and trends. All input data is appreciated and considered. All of us are smarter than any one of us.

8.5.2. Corrective action

Techno-Systems, Inc. takes corrective action to eliminate the cause of non-conformities in order to prevent their recurrence. Corrective actions are appropriate to the non-conformities encountered.

These actions include:

- identifying non-conformities.
- determining the causes of non-conformity.
- evaluating the need for action to ensure that the non-conformities do not recur.
- determining and implementing the action needed.
- recording the results of the action taken.
- the reviewing of the corrective action taken.

8.5.3. Preventive action

Techno-Systems, Inc. determines action to eliminate the causes of potential non-conformities to prevent occurrence. Preventive actions anticipate effects of the potential problems.

These actions include:

- determining potential non-conformities and their causes.
- evaluating the need for action to prevent the occurrence of non-conformities.
- determining and implementing the action needed.
- recording the results of the action taken.
- the reviewing of the preventive action taken.

(last page)

Appendix

Kevin said, "This extra page was added at end of the Quality Manual that I borrowed. It's not part of the ISO Standards, but I like it and would like to work it into our Quality System. What do you think of this, Bill?"

(optional extra page)

Quality Management Principles

1. Customer-focused organization: Take great pride in meeting customer requirements, don't reward yourself for simply following procedures. You depend on your customers so you should understand their requirements and strive to exceed customer expectations.

2. Leadership: Continual improvement and customer satisfaction are more successful when led by top management. Leaders provide direction and make sure all are on course. Lead by positive example.

3. Involvement of people: People, not machines, make quality a reality. When vision, objectives and plans are shared, everyone will be working together to benefit the organization. All of us are smarter than any one of us.

4. Process approach: Organize work the way it naturally flows. When activities are linked together there is a structure for effectively managing and improvement.

5. System approach to management: Grouping processes creates a system. Top management organizes the processes into a system to meet requirements of customers and interested parties.

6. Continual improvement: To achieve excellence, never settle for status quo; continue to make things better. Set your organization apart.

7. Factual approach to decision making: Make decisions based on the facts. There is a reason for everything.

8. Mutually beneficial supplier relationships: Treat suppliers as business partners, not as adversaries. You depend on suppliers so you should work toward a win/win situation.

9. Always be honest: When dealing with anybody, your customers, your suppliers, your employees, yourself, all people, always be honest.

Even little white lies can escalate and will probably come back to haunt you.

10. Create and foster an environment of mutual respect: The "Golden Rule."

"I like that last page too. What do you think Patti?" said Bill.

"It really says a lot. I know, from my personal standpoint, I'm going to ask for more ideas from everyone involved with any new projects. I probably lost my patience a couple of times after I took over the company from Denny. Kevvy, I apologize if I ever offended you when I should have been asking questions. I just didn't want to be asking any dumb questions."

"There's no such thing as a dumb question, Patti," said Kevin for about the millionth time in his life. What he really wanted to add, probably in part because he hated her calling him "Kevvy" was: "only dumb people who ask questions," but he didn't.

"Kevin, why is there a question mark where the *Quality Policy* is supposed to be? How about if we plug in our *Mission Statement?*" Bill asked.

"It's not that easy and if it was, it wouldn't be as effective. For one thing, even though they're sort of related and definitely linked, the Quality policy is to provide interested parties and our own employees our vision for our products or services, the Mission Statement is more like a company slogan."

"Can't you just write one anyway?"

"I probably could, with Patti's help, but the Quality Policy should be well thought out, original and come from the top people. I suppose the Quality Management Team would be best for us. We're supposed to think 'holistically' about our business and articulate how our vision for the future will meet our business objectives and satisfy our customers. ISO actually considers the Quality Policy a 'document' and describes in detail how it should be written."

"Wow! They don't miss a thing, do they?" Patti commented.

Kevin shuffled some papers, "here's what I was looking for." He paused and said, "I've got the ISO 9001:2000 requirements right here." Kevin passed out copies.

Those requirements ensure that the document:

- is appropriate to the purpose of the organization;

- includes a commitment to comply with requirements and continually improve the effectiveness of the Quality Management System;

- provides a framework for establishing and reviewing quality objectives;

- is communicated and understood within the organization; and

- is reviewed for continuing suitability.

Kevin had added some common quality objectives that organizations measure:

- customer satisfaction (and perception);

- on time delivery of products and services; and

- product conformity results.

"The policy should be kept short, demonstrate product quality and be cross-functional across the organization," said Kevin.

"Thanks, Kevin. We'll add it to the quality team agenda for our next meeting."

"Oh, before I forget. Every page in the manual with the exception of the cover page and the 'Quality Management Principles' page would have an information block, and/or a header, and/or a footer containing this info." Kevin ticked off:

- Techno-Systems, Inc.

- Page number

- Revision number or "0"

- Date of revision or original date

Both Patti and Bill were absolutely amazed over how much Kevin had accomplished in such a short time frame. Neither knew that he had it in him to be so organized. Sure, he was good at what he did or he wouldn't be doing it, but this was his "finest hour," so to speak, so far. Bill seemed more impressed than Patti.

"Out of curiosity, if we were providing a service instead of a product, how would our manual look?" Bill asked.

"Strangely enough, the wording would obviously be different but I'm kind of certain the same ISO principles would apply. Any processes, for products or service, would have a similar need for setting, implementing and monitoring the initial and ongoing quality needs. The ISO information I've read seems intentionally vague in the specific action required but then I've only researched ISO 9000 info. I stumbled onto standards for a testing laboratory and the words were different but the concept was pretty close. I guess I'd contact the ASQ, the American Society for Quality, visit their website or something.

"Thanks Kevin, if we ever have an additional need, we'll do just that but for now, this looks almost perfect the way it is," gushed Bill. "It's a perfect guide for us to grow Techno-Systems from all sorts of angles.

"Well, the word 'perfect' in the world of inspection, especially nowadays, is not a word to be taken lightly," said Kevin, "but thank you." "Patti do you have any questions?"

"No Kevin. It looks good though. I'd be more excited but this has got to be the craziest week in my life, and it's not over. I'm just sorry we didn't look at this years ago."

"I know what you mean, but, better now than never. Do you folks have a couple more minutes?" Patti was getting antsy.

Bill said he did and Patti nodded her head.

"Great. You guys have been really patient with this, uh, not so exciting stuff."

"Well, Kevin," said Bill, "for everything else going on right now, you've gotten my attention and shown again how focused you are. You're an asset."

"That reminds me of a guy who lived over a bank; his assets over millions." quipped Kevin.

Bill chuckled. Patti smiled and said, "cute, Kevin."

Kevin blushed. He also thought Patti was a fox and kind of hot. "So, last point," he said. "I found this on a blog."

Kevin had read a tip on how to make the transition easier. He explained how a lot of people felt threatened by change so they preferred, at some level, to see change fail. It's an uphill battle if those involved don't have their hearts in it. The solution is to have as many as possible make it their own project by making them a part of its success. Having informational meetings upfront and early in the project helped. Most people want to be part of the team and to be successful in team goals.

If they buy into the benefits to the team through success by the company, they'll be more apt to make it work. They'll help instead of hinder, all through the process. Compiling data and doing audits, initial, registration, internal and surveillance, will go smoother. The persons using the system will actually write much of their own work instructions and then the ISO coordinator simply reformats the data for the documentation. Say what you do; do what you say.

"Ownership. That's the key to total company acceptance and positive participation," said Kevin.

"Thank you Kevin. Let's make it happen," said Bill, "and on that note, let's finish-up for the day, get out of here on time tonight."

While the very best feature of an ISO program was the way it facilitated corrective action, thought Kevin, the internal audit system was pretty cool too. A third party registrar would come in for the initial certification of compliance to ISO 9001:2000 Standards and the subsequent annual surveillance audits to perpetuate certification. That didn't apply to Techno-Systems though, at least not until they sought formal certification. Anyway, internal audits were different from third party audits in that they were conducted by Techno-Systems' own personnel each year to make sure the company was following the standards in the prescribed manner.

An internal audit system, initially set up by the Quality Management Team (QMT) with predetermined questions, unknown to the areas or departments to be audited, would be carried out independently by the Internal Audit Team. The individual questions would be posed by Internal Audit Team members who were *not* directly part of the area or department being audited for obvious reasons. You can't expect an auditor to be unbiased if they're reviewing their own work.

For example, someone from the shipping department might be assigned the purchasing department and both parties might learn something to improve their view of the overall operation. Or, someone from an office position could better understand the manufacturing function by auditing them. A win/win situation and verification of the quality system. Two for the price of one. A twofer.

It not only identified non-compliance issues, it also identified complying areas for praise and possible bragging rights. All of the personnel in the QMT would have a feeling of importance and more like part of the greater whole. The QMT personnel would be rotated every year to give *everyone* the opportunity to participate.

Other benefits to the internal audits' program were the slick transitions to the more formal Registrar Audit if and when they were needed. A little practice and experience can ease the pressures of an initial certification audit performed by outsiders and make all concerned more comfortable. A major point to keep in mind is *the registrar audits to pass, not to fail.* The registrar wants to work with you, Kevin understood, to get you certified and then maintain that certification through annual surveillance audits, which, if the initial registrar performs the audits regularly, is like an annuity to them. Ask the registrar for a pre-assessment of your QMS, a dry run of the quality system compliance, and listen closely to their suggestions. You'll know exactly what you need to do.

6

The SBA

Friday morning and Bill was expecting the representative from the Small Business Administration shortly. What a week of mixed emotion, he thought. Denny, Patti, the possible opportunity from Systems-Plus, the police and ISO, all within one week. And besides all that, the month's total shipping dollars was going to be the third highest in the company history, highest since Bill took over the reins.

Bill had thought for a fleeting minute that he didn't need government business right now. He just as quickly decided that it was still a good time to pursue it because he wouldn't be under any stress to accept a contract. The best time to go after new business was before you really needed it, allowing for more viable options. And, if what Bill heard was true, the government may be repairing present equipment rather than buying brand new for awhile. He had also just read that there was "a huge difference between a large business and a small business, and what's required of them. Too many small businesses are afraid of the federal government because they think there are all these rules and regulations that, in fact, don't apply to them."

Large businesses could handle more rules and regulations simply because they had more personnel to do it. Companies like Techno-Systems didn't have that luxury, or even a diminished level of paperwork. Three or two or even one person pretty much did it all in a smaller business. In part for that reason, Bill had decided to utilize the SBA, the PTAC, and any other assistance he might find.

Yes, Bill thought, it's a good time to try it from all the different angles he could think of right now. He decided his long-term goal would be from

25 percent to 30 percent of his business volume, down from initially but still substantial.

At 10 o'clock, Rosemary Haberberg, the SBA representative, arrived right on time at Techno-System's lobby, a good sign to Bill. After accepting a cup of black coffee, she sat down and wanted to get down to business. She seemed like a pleasant person and had a very professional demeanor. Bill felt an immediate confidence in her, even before she spoke.

"Mr. Nelson. May I call you Bill?"

"Sure. I wish you would," he replied.

"Good. Please call me Rose. Everybody else does. I took the liberty to look-up Techno-Systems in our manufacturing directory database. It's good to see you're an established business. Have you tried for government contracts before?"

"No, this is our first time. Is it even possible to become a new supplier to Uncle Sam these days?"

"Yes, although it takes something to get the Contract Officer's attention though. If you had only just started a business and didn't have anything special, it would be pretty tough. As it is, I understand that you have a very good reputation and that's important. Your commercial track record may suffice if it's as good as I believe your history is."

"As far as I know, this company has done fairly well, and our quality has never been an issue. What does the government primarily look for?"

"A positive history, an ability to demonstrate good quality in both products and services, financial stability and solid management skills. The government wants to know you can deliver what you said you could. If you can't, you may be liable if someone else has to do it for you. You pretty much have to be able to hold your own in a competitive marketplace, have you conducted international business?"

"Yes we have. In fact, we're setting up an ISO 9001:2000-like Quality System that should make us more credible in that arena in the future."

"ISO-like?" asked Rose.

"For now, yes. Our Quality Assurance Department is setting it up in such a way to pursue actual registration at a later date. For one thing, I understand it can cost about $60,000 for a company our size."

"I've heard that. One way around a formal quality program right away is to do subcontracting for a prime contractor. A good quality program also helps with them as well. Primes have a lot of companies vying for their business. A subcontractor has to stand out from the crowd."

"I don't doubt that," said Bill. "By the way, I visited the SBA website and couldn't believe how much good, free information you have available. The same with our PTAC."

"Thank you, Bill," said Rose. "It's important for us at the SBA to not only be your partner and your advocate, but also to be the agency that you count on to respond to your needs."

Rose went on to share other pearls of information regarding the SBA and tips regarding contracting with the federal government. Last year, the SBA provided financial, technical and management assistance to help Americans start, run and grow their businesses to over a million small businesses. SBA negotiates small business goals for each federal agency buying products or services. Under the Small Business Act, federal agencies reserve a variety of procurements, called "set-asides," exclusively for small businesses.

Prime contractors are required to make a "best effort" attempt to use small businesses as subcontractors on contracts that exceed $100,000. While prime contractors are awarded huge dollar contracts every year, approximately 95 percent of 11 million contracts written were for $100,000 or less. On average, the federal government seeks to award 23 percent of its procurements to small businesses. Small businesses have extraordinary contracting opportunities from the federal government because they set goals to purchase from small businesses, encourage large prime companies to subcontract portions of government contracts to small businesses and outsourcing services. There will be even more opportunities in the future for businesses doing the kind of public services that the federal government is outsourcing to save money.

The SBA contends that contracting with the federal government is not hard or complicated, *if* you take the time to learn the rules and you follow the regulations. Somewhere between the ugly, outdated rumors denigrating government contracting and the cakewalk implied by some government agencies, you will find the reality of selling to the United States Federal Government.

Bill asked if the rumor was true that a Request For Proposal, or RFP, being offered by the government was not worth even considering. And that the situation was that the Contracting Officer had already made up their mind for the supplier but had to get three bids anyway. Bill understood it could make for an expensive exercise, in time and money, with no benefit to the second or third bidders.

"You should check with your PTAC if you see a suspect request," answered Rose, sort of sidestepping the question. Her answer was probably what Bill would do if he saw an RFP that he couldn't resist. Much later though, Bill was to look up other peoples experiences with RFP's and found this in a blog: "RFP's are notorious for being biased. It is well understood by most vendors that, if you did not participate to helping build the RFP (by way of previous discussions about your solution or even writing the thing yourself) then you are not likely to win it. And, for the record, making the cut in the first or second round does *not* necessarily mean anything, but is many times just a way for the customer to bide their time (for whatever reason: budget, internal issues, etc.) before making the 'official decision.'" Bill would just contact his PTAC anyway to be sure.

Rose glossed over some of the more well known programs supported by the SBA. She explained how government agencies are required to establish and strive to meet goals to benefit specific company types. Besides the "small business" designation, which seemed quite liberal to Bill for maximum size requirements, businesses received preferential consideration if they were owned a minimum of 51 percent by a woman, veteran or service-disabled veteran. A small disadvantaged business (SBD) was defined as being operated by a person or persons, socially and economically disadvantaged, or 51 percent or more minority-owned.

"An 8(a) designated company has advantages although in many cases, an SBD is just as effective, especially from a subcontracting point of view," she said, adding, "and the SBD doesn't take near as long."

"Bill, did you know that Techno-Systems is located in a HUBZone?"

"I heard a while back that we probably were, but I'm not sure what it means."

"For starters, it means you have an advantage over a lot of your competition on certain contracts you may be quoting. The HUBZone Program, or Historically Underutilized Business Zone, is designed to promote economic development and employment growth in distressed areas by providing access to more federal contracting opportunities. We can certify Techno-Systems as a HUBZone business. You can visit our website for the details but the bottom line, oversimplified, is, you could be up to 10 percent higher on price and still be awarded the contract. In theory, the disadvantages, or advantages, I've mentioned are cumulative, but read the bid carefully and double-check with someone if you're not sure. It's not always exactly clear."

"Great Rose. I deserved a break today. Thank you."

"You are entirely welcome, it's what we do. But, again, please keep in mind that you can't arbitrarily count on flat price advantages when you're quoting. Much of the time you'll have the price history on a procurement and you'll have to read between the lines if the history doesn't always make sense."

Bill was thinking that what Rose just said didn't totally make sense either although he made a mental note to use discretion when reviewing price histories.

"You know, Rose," Bill said, "I'm feeling better about pursuing government business. The more I check into it, the more I feel like the government is genuinely trying to make it easier to do business with them. The SBA and our PTAC are very helpful."

"We are trying. I enjoy working with a business like yours where you're sincere, above-board and eager to follow the rules. Not everyone does. Not often, at least I think, people have represented their company falsely. They're always caught and end-up paying a fine or being imprisoned, or both."

"Not an issue with us. We're squeaky clean," said Bill, thinking, but not saying anything, about the Dennis Bell problems.

Rose wrapped-up her presentation by giving Bill a resource directory, information on SCORE, upcoming workshops and other data for him to read later.

Bill thanked her and walked her to the front door with assurances that he would call her if and when he had any questions.

Bill was secretly flattered when Patti seemed more interested in the "SBA guy" than in the benefit's the SBA had to offer Techno-Systems. He got the distinct impression that Patti was jealous because of the questions she asked about Rose. Maybe it was because of Bill's office being kind of their *special* place after last week.

Late last Friday, Patti and Bill were talking about business when the conversation became more personal and then turned downright intimate. After they both admitted to unfulfilled sex lives recently, Bill commented that it sure wasn't Patti's physical attributes being a factor in her diminished love life and then went on to explain why he felt that way. Patti reciprocated with a glowing review of all the positives she saw in Bill. One thing led to another as such things tend to do and they corrected the lack of sex issue right there on Bill's office floor.

So maybe that was it, thought Bill. I'll never have another woman, other than Patti in my office with the door closed again. Bill did have his door shut now to go over the payroll and there was a soft knock on the door. It must be Patti he thought and took a deep breath before saying, in what he thought was his most provocative voice, "Come in."

"Hi Bill, got a minute?'

It was Jeremy with a machined part in his hand so Bill sighed and just looked at Jeremy for a second, then said, "Hello Jeremy, can I help you?"

"Did I come at a bad time? We've got a slight problem with the rolled threads in this aluminum casting. It's just barely okay, but I wanted to clear it with you because you spoke to the customer about this part once before."

"No, no, it's a good time. What have we got?" Bill asked, holding his hand out for the part in question.

Bill made a suggestion and was glad that Jeremy had the foresight to ask as that particular account was red flagged on marginal quality. Jeremy was a seasoned manufacturing supervisor who had come up through the ranks and gotten to where he was by being a good machinist. Besides being hard to B.S. because he was experienced, he was able to communicate what he knew to the people who worked under him.

Some supervisors are promoted to their position when they're able to produce better, more, and in less time than their coworkers. The standard theory being that all the others will learn to do everything the same way for the same successes. The problem can arise if the supervisor is not able to communicate those winning techniques.

It sure wasn't a problem with Jeremy though, even if might have had some other secret quirks. He apparently had the whole package: communication skills, empathy, technical expertise, a positive attitude, *and* he was hard to B.S. when employees came to him with lame excuses. Jeremy, Kevin, Bill Sexton, Patti and Bill Nelson comprised the newly formed Quality Management Team. All of the team members had many of Jeremy's attributes and could handle the quality system issues besides their regular duties. Larger companies with an ISO system were usually structured differently although all companies, regardless of size, did what they had to do to satisfy the ISO Quality Management System requirements.

A one person company, Bill understood, would have just one person wearing all of the different hats necessary to conduct business and to satisfy the requirements. If that was the case, the same name would appear wherever and whenever it's formally requested. An example could be the CCR registration form over the internet, the same name would be used for all of the different fields as the POC (Point of Contact). In fact, Patti mentioned an option on the form to complete most of the fields with the same name by clicking the appropriate spot. It must be pretty common, thought Bill.

Bill had read that while it may be tempting to over-inflate a company's apparent size by fudging and using a variety of names for positions, it wouldn't fool anyone. Besides not working because these guys have seen it all, it could be illegal if a company got a contract and the exaggeration was discovered while verifying data for fulfillment of requirements. The best policy is to always be completely honest with *everybody* and the government is far from being an exception. Very far.

7

Finding Opportunities

Bill considered delegating the prospecting function to someone else and then he reconsidered, thinking, if he didn't know exactly what he might be looking for, what should he expect from them? Techno-Systems was basically a job shop, albeit a highly technical one, that made product usually based on their customer's requirements. He could utilize Techno-Systems' present facility and capacity list, maybe Systems-Plus' too someday, but he wanted to stay open on new, different equipment they could justify with a government contract as well. With that in mind, he decided to do it himself for now.

Bill went to his state's PTAC website to check their resources and hit the jackpot. There was an upcoming seminar on "Contracting 101" later that week. It was being held in a city almost 250 miles away but the next basic seminar was over a month later. A more specific seminar for machining and fabrication was scheduled three months from now though Bill really just needed to get started immediately. He was right in thinking that he would get more out of the more advanced seminar he if learned what to look for by then.

One of Bill's commercial customers was located only 15 miles from where the seminar was being held in the morning so he decided to kill two birds with one stone and call on them that same afternoon. Bill secured registration with the PTAC, called his customer and hit the jackpot again by making a late lunch appointment. He then decided to go for the "hat trick" and checked another customer he could visit later that afternoon. The buyer was not going to be there but the assistant buyer would be. Better yet, thought Bill. It would be a long day but it was a good time to get out of the office. Sort of a "mental health" day.

Bill went to the FedBizOpps website, or Federal Business Opportunities. As usual, he found a wealth of information at his fingertips. He had decided to check it out before he attended the basic seminar. Again, learn a little bit so his questions at the seminar would have a little more weight to him personally.

The most prominent feature he found on the Homepage was this statement:

> "FedBizOpps.gov is the single government point-of-entry (GPE) for Federal government procurement opportunities over $25,000. Government buyers are able to publicize their business opportunities by posting information directly to FedBizOpps via the internet. Through one portal-FedBizOpps (FBO)—commercial vendors seeking Federal markets for their products and services can search, monitor and retrieve opportunities solicited by the entire Federal contracting community."

There were features for "Quick Search" and "Advanced Search" although Bill wanted to explore as much as possible. He clicked on "Vendors", found a few options, clicked on the "Find Business Opportunity 'go'" and found even more options.

Very interesting, thought Bill. You could customize your search to filter out the bids that you were definitely *not* interested in viewing. He clicked on a few filters and clicked on "Start Search". Whoa! Way too many. He went back a couple of pages and considered the "Related Links" on the right hand side of the page then clicked on "Demo FBO".

The demo didn't take long and soon Bill was again back to the "Find Business Opportunities" page. Under "Search by Set-Aside Code" he tried "Total HUBzone" and later tried "Total Small Business", both under the "All Days" filter. Still way too many, thought Bill when he noticed how far back in time that particular filter could take him. The requests were obviously still open although Bill decided that there could be some issues with the older ones and planned on spending his valuable time on more current opportunities.

His plan was to check out the more Techno-Systems specific opportunities first and, time permitting on any particular day, he would check out more distant type opportunities. Also, he would check FedBizOpps every three days or so. Otherwise it would take longer to explore everything and the FBO system had a three day option. That was the plan for after the seminar by the PTAC anyway. For now, Bill had to get caught up if he was going to be gone for a whole day.

Ten days later, everything was going along fine in Bill's world. The seminar gave him a lot of ideas. It might have saved Patti a little time for when she completed the CCR registration but only if the seminar had been closer to work. So, overall, Bill was good to go for now and would attend the more advanced seminar later if he had time. There was a possibility of delegating the prospecting duty to someone else, and that person could attend. Bill had a "brain fart" regarding someone from the company, familiar with the operation, doing the searches from their own home. It could be like a part-time job for an interested person and then only if they could agree on a fair compensation.

Whatever, Bill had too many other things happening to give it too much thought right now. The biggest thing, by far, was the investigation into Denny's murder. Both Patti and Bill were each questioned again as the detectives came up with the queries and they both were still not considered as being involved. All of the Systems-Plus employees were interviewed at least once and a few of Techno-Systems' employees as well. Neither Patti nor Bill had heard anything really definite about the case.

Bill was still interested in buying-out Systems-Plus lock, stock and barrel although he figured if he pushed too much right now, it could look suspicious. He'd hold back asking about the future of Dennis' old company for awhile.

His relationship with Patti was improving, of course their having sex had been a fairly good icebreaker. She was still working with him or under him every day and while they weren't outwardly dating yet, they shared another common bond. Patti did have more knowledge of the inner-workings of Techno-Systems than anyone else in the company, with the exception of Bill. He was wary of being seen too much with her in public until Denny's murder settled down a bit. Bill thought that might look suspicious for the same reason as he didn't want to ask too many question about the disposition of Systems-Plus.

Another issue was the feeling of hypocrisy Bill felt over his condemnation of interoffice sexual humor and flirting in a memo he had posted just a few months before Patti came back. In it, he had cautioned against any behavior or jokes that may have to be repeated in a court of law if they had offended anyone enough to file a lawsuit. What seems funny at the time usually wouldn't in a formal courtroom. What prompted his chastisement was a cute joke that went too far.

All of the guys liked to see Bambi lean over when she wore a low-cut top. Situations were subtly staged by a couple of the more seemingly desperate ones like Kevin, even though he was happily married. Kevin and some guy named Dave had discovered that Bambi usually parked her car right under the second story lunchroom window. When she was wearing dresses everyday, a car had once parked close to her driver's door and when she left for the day, she had to climb through the passenger door and over the console between the seats. True, the resultant view was spectacular with her great legs and a flash of panty. Bambi, as usual, had no idea of what had happened because she was a truly innocent and good person.

She probably thought it was an incredible coincident that every couple of weeks someone would park too close again. To Bill's shame, and in a weaker moment, he himself had once jockeyed for position at the lunchroom window until one day, when she had worn a short skirt and brief panties. Innocent Patti had hiked up her skirt and paused while straddling the console and the later observation that she must not have been a real blond was a hot topic for days. Bill put the kibosh on the not-so-cute-anymore peepshow.

Techno-Systems certainly didn't need a sexual harassment lawsuit right now, or any other time for that matter. The potentially serious situation prompted Bill to reiterate their policy against such matters with a flurry of memos and posters condemning future activity which could be remotely construed as sexual in nature. Bambi apparently heard though the office grapevine that she had been a victim but Patti was able to smooth it over this time. Patti said there wouldn't be another time and Bambi was forgiving, this time only.

Hmm, thought Bill. A man is murdered and another man is interested in the victim's wife *and* his business. In a way, it was just a coincidence. He smiled when he thought of a joke Denny had told him, "Coincidence is when you, your wife, and your alarm clock all go off at the same time." Then he wondered if *that* was a coincidence or an irony. Bill couldn't help but think of Patti again before getting back on the FedBizOpps' website.

Bill had started out his prospecting according to his plan of checking out all the open bid requests pertaining to his interests for the last three weeks. If he was disciplined enough, he would only have to go back for the three days option in the future. Bill learned a little bit more every time he went to the FBO website. The PTAC had searching ideas that Bill probably wouldn't have found on his own although he found that he could also now look at a bid request and mentally filter them down faster than when he first started. There were buzzwords and other information he could pick-out almost peripherally as he perused the pages.

Bill knew that the less obvious potential bid sources he had learned about at the last seminar and the sources he would learn about later could yield tremendous opportunities, but he'd pursue them in more depth in a couple of months. Bill had made a commitment to give this endeavor at least a year. He knew that going after business like gangbusters for a couple of months and then giving up if his unrealistic expectations were not met right away wouldn't say too much for good planning. Better to make the commitment upfront and build on it as he went along.

Patience and persistence. Patience and persistence. That would be his mantra, his rallying cry until he received his first electronic payment from the government. Without the firm commitment, he'd be better off putting his energies someplace else. To be awarded a contract within a few months is very unlikely, though his goal was to get a contract within the first year. If he didn't, he would probably keep trying for at least another year. Bill also understood the odds were against him getting the first contract he bid on, but he accepted that.

Visiting the FedBizOpps website on a regular basis and other computer searching would probably be the type of prospecting Bill would use most often at first. That's not to say it would be the most productive though. Some federal agencies had their own seminars. Some of the states sponsored conferences specifically for exposing opportunities. Some other conferences or symposiums produced opportunities. All of these presented the vendor with a chance to meet personally with buyers.

A good reason to personally meet with a buyer is always ideal, but Bill heard that many Government Buyers were difficult to establish relationships with. To just arbitrarily make a sales call on a buyer would usually be a waste of time for all concerned, if you even actually spoke to anyone. Telephone sales calls are not encouraged either for the same reason. Bill knew from firsthand experience about ill-planned sales calls on Techno-Systems being ineffective because they usually just wasted his time. Hell, even some of the receptionists acted offended because he hadn't had an appointment the last time he had made any cold-calls himself. No more of that nowadays.

A whole bunch of years back, the classic cigar smoking salesman would go out and press the flesh, glad-hand his way through most sales calls. Now, you wouldn't want to smell like smoke, it's "salesperson" not "salesman" and appointments are usually needed, if you can get one. It was a "catch 22" that you can't see anyone without an appointment and you can't get an appointment without seeing someone.

Bill supposed you could contact a Contracting Officer if you had any legitimate reasons, like an important question. From what he had heard, you didn't want to contact the contracting office with a question you shouldn't have to ask, something you could learn from the internet, SBA or your PTAC. In fact, the contracting officer was probably the last avenue of explanation for questions, unless it directly pertained to that particular contract.

This adds more time to my expectations of meeting personally with buyers, thought Bill. It wasn't insurmountable, but it will take finesse because these Contracting Officers have probably seen and heard it all, like other professional purchasing people. I'll have to....

"Bill, I have to talk to you," said Patti from his doorway. "I just got word on Denny. The police have decided that Denny committed suicide."

"No!"

"Yes. There hasn't been anything new lately so I called Detective Phelps, you know, and the case was transferred to another cop, Meadows. He was here the first time."

"Oh yeah. He didn't say much, but suicide? How was he supposed to manage that? He was tied up and must have been unconscious."

"The theory is," replied Patti, "he used some sort of slip knots on his hands after he tied his feet. They analyzed some drug I can't pronounce in his system. The amount was all screwed up because of the way he bled out, it goofed up his liver or something."

"Pretty farfetched. So they're saying he was conscious when he tied himself up, then he took enough drugs to pass out?"

"I guess so, but I had a hard time getting a word in edgewise with the new cop."

"I suppose it's possible but it sounds damn improbable. Why did they take Detective Phelps off the case?"

"She had to go back to Wisconsin on an emergency to take care of her elderly parents. She once told me her mother was dangerously forgetful and her dad was just plain demented. I guess it's pretty sad. She's putting them in a home and settling their meager estate. She even asked if I wanted a couple of cats," said Patti.

"Well," said Bill, "I didn't want to say anything but I'm thinking about trying to buy the business assets of Denny's company, Systems-Plus. Hell, the name isn't even that far from Techno-Systems and the people and equipment would fit right in."

"Coincidently, I've been thinking about it too. I'm still flush with money although I don't relish the management part again. Nah, I really don't want to jump out of the frying pan, and besides, I like working with you, Bill."

"Thank you. I enjoy being with you too. It's unlikely too many people would want to assume all of the start-up debt the business is still carrying.

It's a different story for me though, because I can just absorb the whole business fairly painlessly."

"Maybe I can help somehow," said Patti. "Denny's lawyer called to see if I'd be interested in our old house. Its got three mortgages on it and the bank wanted to deal."

"Are you interested in the house?"

"No."

"If you're free for a casual dinner meeting tonight, we can discuss it over an early meal after work."

Patti said, "it's a date."

Bill had two telephone calls he had to make before he could get back to finding opportunities. Two phone calls turned into a half-dozen. Then a quote to take care of <u>right</u> <u>now</u>! Then Kevin came in with a quality discrepancy. The sprinkler company came in to do their annual system check and Bill passed that off to Jeremy. Finally, he sat back down to his computer.

Okay. Finding opportunities. Bill had already been calling on prime contractors as part of his regular commercial business. Of course, now he looked at them differently. At the PTAC seminar, prime contractors were hyped as one way to do federal business without being exposed to the full complexity of the government market. The only difference was instead of the customer being commercial, they would be a prime contractor and Bill would be a subcontractor. As such, Techno-Systems could be a part of the biggest deals. He wondered if working with established primes would rub off on Techno-Systems, kind of like the "halo effect." Maybe he could share their halo for some good PR.

Some of the products that Techno-Systems produced were esoteric to their industry. If Bill could develop anything proprietary, a history with a prime could possibly open doors that commercial history couldn't. One of Bill's friends owned a medium size construction company and, because he was a veteran, had landed a subcontracting job in Afghanistan. On his own, he wouldn't have stood a chance in that no-bid market.

The friend with the construction company had actually been talking to a buyer about a different job and found out the buyer was also the small business liaison. In that capacity, his job was to find small firms to help them meet the terms of their contracts, part of which was utilizing veterans. "The rest is history," his friend had said.

"Subcontracting," friend Mohammed added, "is perfect for my company. While I feel proud of working indirectly with this great government, I have no interest in doing all of the paperwork, only in doing an exceptional job."

And for his company, it was perfect. He won, the prime contractor won and the end user won because Mohammed really did do an exceptional job.

Bill would like to try both, subcontracting and contracting direct, if the opportunity presented itself. Bill actually gave it a shot earlier but came to the conclusion that perhaps subcontracting wasn't always a shortcut to his goal.

There were specific websites highlighting subcontracting, teaming and partnering, but Bill didn't have the feeling that people would be beating a path to his door any time soon. First, it was an incredibly competitive market for companies like Techno-Systems unless you really stood out from the crowd. Bill had done an internet search for "Prime Contractors" and found lists for each state. Easy right? The lists proved to be outdated and, when the information was accurate, the published names were inundated with starry-eyed subcontracting hopefuls from all over the state, the country, the world.

Bill had been pleasantly surprised when he first found a prime he hadn't even heard of was located in a nearby city. Well, that particular prime made it clear to "not waste either's time" by calling again. Bill decided, even if they hadn't displayed the subtlety of an elephant's reproductive organ, they would have still been totally devoid of basic courtesy.

Some of the other primes Bill sent emails to as a "pre-approach" and then telephoned were as different as night and day compared to the neighboring prime. True professionals, they were gracious and accommodating, unfortunately while telling Bill the same thing. That wasn't entirely fair because a few had specific web pages just for aspiring subcontractors and Bill had a feeling some of those might contact him sometime. One of the Small Business Liaison's comments actually encouraged him.

Bill recalled over thirty years ago when his father, Randall Nelson, had worked for a subcontractor. Funny, he thought, my dad was involved in some of the same stuff I'm working on although my dad was a machine operator at All Steel Specialties in Capitol City at the time. Bill hadn't thought about this in years.

All Steel Specialties was a metals distributor that was contacted by a huge prime because they had the facilities to buy large steel coils in truckload quantities and process them down to a condition and quantity needed by a smaller manufacturer. The prime—Hey, technically Techno-Systems will be a prime too if we get a contract-—was looking for a company to purchase Hot Rolled Pickled and Oiled (HRP&O Bill remembered) steel coil, slit it to width, roll it down a couple of thousands (his dad's job), and emboss it with a small diamond pattern for fragmentation (also his dad's job).

The small rolling mill was government property, loaned to All Steel for the duration of the contract apparently but the embossing mill was purchased by All Steel Specialties and would pay for itself on the prime's contract and be used later for embossing materials for fishing lures (cool).

All Steel supplied the embossed steel coil to a tube manufacturer that formed it into a continuous welded seam tube, embossed side in, then cut into twenty foot long lengths. The tube manufacturer then sent the tubing to the prime to be cut into short lengths, stamped to a bullet shape on one end and machined on the other end for a cap to be installed.

The bullet shaped component was then supplied to another subcontractor to be packed with explosive material and fitted with a fuse for ignition. The resultant subassembly was fitted to another subassembly making the completed component a projectile.

The weapon system used to deliver the projectile in the field was also the responsibility of the prime and was undoubtedly subcontracted out as well. Randall Nelson didn't know anything about that although the prime's facilitator had clued him in on what happened to the embossed raw material.

However, Bill did remember his dad agonizing over being even a small part in a system designed to hurt people although, as Randall's supervisor pointed out, his country *was* at war and this product could save his countrymen's lives. He also pointed out that young Bill could be one of those lives saved. As a matter of fact, Ray, Randall's brother who was a veteran of Korea, was clearly proud of Randall's wartime contribution to the Vietnam War.

And that was just one contract from a long time ago. Coincidently, Bill did join the Army after trying college for one year and deciding that college wasn't for him. Fortunately Bill served his military time during a period of relative peace and then attended a machine tool program at a technical school.

Bill found an old list of standard questions to ask yourself before trying to be a subcontractor. The list was dated from over ten years ago but was still applicable and seemed geared to people not necessarily interested in becoming a prime contractor themselves. He thought that because he had already answered some of the questions when he first considered the federal marketplace. If nothing else, the list was a good review:

- Is there anyway to set my company apart from the competition? (There's a lot of good competition out there).

- What are your company's main strengths and weaknesses? (Be realistic).

- What are your customer service strengths and weaknesses?

- Where is your company most efficient and cost effective?

- How well known are you within your industry? (Be the leading edge).

- Can you demonstrate to a prime that your products or services are of the highest quality? (Having a good Quality Manual isn't enough).

- Can you provide support for your products or services?

- Can you meet deadlines? (Your competition will).

- Can you handle unusual rules and regulatory red tape? (May trickle down).

- Will subcontracting take resources away from your existing customers?

- Is there someone within the company who can be the lead contact with a prime? (An assigned liaison).

Bill tried to be honest in his self-analyzing evaluation, mostly because if he wasn't, he'd only be trying to fool himself. No future in that.

"Hey, Hey, Mr. Bill." It was Bill Sexton at his door again. Bill S. was a fifty-something notoriously known happy guy. He preferred to be called plain "Bill" to differentiate the two Bills (Bill N. secretly thought of him as B.S.), but everybody called him "Six-ten" though not because of his height. Six-ten was started by Kevin, who decided Bill S. looked like the hands of a clock at 6:10, because he was bent from the waist to his left. It should have been 6:02 as Bill wasn't bent that much but it didn't sound right and would have taken more than a little vowel movement. Poor Bill had been in a nasty car accident years ago, not only giving him his name-sake but a truly distinctive face as well. Kids seemed to like him, perhaps because he always appeared to be leaning towards them to hear them better.

"Hi Bill," said Bill N. "What's up?"

"What up is I've got problem with the plastic handles from BestCo that just came in. They're more orange than red. Probably not a big deal but they sure don't match the knobs. I know you're pushing this assembly out otherwise I would have already sent them back."

"I'm pushing here because they're pushing there, but they still have to be to spec. We could field-install them but it's a can of worms. Call Bestco and get the right ones coming Premium Express.

"I'm on it," said Bill S. and turned to go.

"Quick minute, could you please come back when you're done?"

"Sure Mr. Bill."

Bill Sexton was responsible for shipping and receiving though Bill Nelson had aspirations for him.

The plans were to make Bill S. in charge of meeting the government's packaging requirements besides his regular duties. It was part of Bill N's grand plans for a company-wide higher level of professionalism by giving key personnel titles and the accompanying accountabilities. Techno-Systems employee's growth and personal advancement were to be linked directly to Techno-System's success.

As it turned out, Bill N. wouldn't see Bill S. until later.

Bill's telephone rang. It was Britney, his thirteen-year old daughter, asking for a ride to the library if he was available. Bill flashed on his "date" with Patti and, regretfully, because it didn't seem like he had any time with the girls during the week, begged off with a promise for some other time.

Britney said, "that's okay dad, earlier mom said she could."

So she actually just wanted an excuse to spend a little more time with me, thought Bill. The older the girls got, the more the divorce seemed to impact them with their daddy only around every other weekend. He sort of wished his ex would remarry for the kid's sake. He also wished she would remarry for the sake of his pocketbook. Child support, okay. Alimony, rather not.

These were important years for Becky and Britney, and Bill really wanted to be there for them but he had to make money to provide for their needs. With guilt promises of college support to wherever they wished, he was building a pretty good sized "nut" for the future. He vowed to figure out someway to be a better father, even at the expense of his work. Bill was thinking about spending more time with the kids when Patti poked her head in and said, "Are you hungry yet? It's almost dinnertime."

Tonight, they didn't dally.

8

Reviewing Requests

Overall, Bill was a happy man. In the seven-months since he had decided to pursue federal government business, his life had changed. Bill had closed his office door, leaned back in his chair, put his feet on the corner of his desk and reflected on the events as they had unfolded:

- Techno-Systems business had been converted to a comfortable (from a scheduling viewpoint anyway) blend of mixed delivery dates.

- He and Patti were enjoying an equally (albeit more satisfying) comfortable relationship. Patti had moved in with him two-months ago.

- Patti had ended-up buying the assets of Systems-Plus with the money she had gotten when she had sold Techno-Systems plus interest earned. They merged.

- Patti and Bill were getting married in two-weeks. Sort of a win/win, double merger, everyone benefits' arrangement.

- Techno-Systems' ISO based Quality System was improving their bottom-line and was a surprising marketing tool. Systems-Plus would be worked-in.

- Exceeded expectations! Techno-Systems had located a perfect Invitation for Bid (IFB) on which to submit a quote.

Of course, not everything could be perfect:

- Bill had to go back to his bank to increase his loans, to increase his working capital, to increase the merged businesses' viability.

- Bill's youngest daughter, Becky, now eleven, had a real problem with Patti becoming her stepmother.

- Detective Meadows, after disappearing for about six-months, all of a sudden was on a personal quest to re-open and close the Dennis Bell case.

Why was Becky acting like she resented Patti, who had already said she wasn't trying to replace Becky's mother. Why after all this time was the case re-opened? Who was this guy, Meadows, and why was he obsessing on Bill and Patti? These questions were distracting but Bill was trying his best to focus the issue at hand, the requests for action on government opportunities.

The first thing Bill did was to carefully read the request. It was actually a suggestion he had heard and had made a mental note of: read everything carefully, and then read it again. The request Bill was perusing included a "Numbered Note", in this case it was 8., which he then reviewed. Numbered notes were a part of almost every listed offering in FedBizOpps because they were stated to avoid the unnecessary repetition of spelling-out the details. It was obviously easier to refer to a digit than to write out a paragraph or two to say the same thing.

Wherever and whenever a Numbered Note was included in a notice, the note referred to must be read as a formal part of the item or section in which it appears. Bill knew he would refer to his "Numbered Notes" in his three-ring binder often so he kept the following copy in the front of his reference material. Even though some of the notes were noted as being deleted, they were still listed for either history or because some die-hard people still used them.

1. The proposed contract is 100% set aside for small business concerns.

2. A portion of the acquisition is set aside for small business concerns.

3. The proposed contract is a labor surplus area set-aside. (This note is deleted as of 7/21/99.)

4. The proposed contract is 100 percent set aside for small disadvantaged business concerns (SDB). Offers from concerns other than SDBs will not be considered. (This note is deleted as of 11/24/99.)

5. The proposed contract is 100% set aside for Historically Black Colleges and Universities (HBCUs) and Minority Institutions (Mis). Offers from other than HBCUs and Mis will not be considered.

6. The proposed contact is a total small disadvantaged business set aside or is being considered as a total small disadvantaged business set aside. (This note is deleted as of 11/24/99.)

7. The proposed contract is 100% set aside for Historically Black Colleges, Universities and Minority Institutions or is partially set aside for Historically Black Colleges, Universities and Minority Institutions.

8. The solicitation document contains information that has been designated as "Militarily Critical Technical Data." Only businesses that have been certified by the Department of Defense, United States/Canada Joint Certification Office, and have a valid requirement may have a copy of the solicitation document. All requests for copies of the solicitation document must include a certified copy of DD Form 2345, Militarily Critical Technical Data Agreement. To obtain certification, contact: Commander, Defense Logistics Information Service (DLIS), ATTN: U.S./Canada Joint Certification Office, 74 Washington Avenue North, Battle Creek, MI 49017-3084 or call the DLIS at (800)-352-3572. The DLIS United States/Canada Joint Certification Lookup service is available via the Internet at: http://www.dlis.dla.mil/ccal/.

9. Interested parties may obtain copies of Military and Federal Specifications and Standards, Qualified Product Lists, Military Handbooks, and other standardization documents from the DoD Single Stock Point (DODSSP), in Philadelphia, PA. Most documents are available in Adobe PDF format from the ASSIST database via the Internet at http://assist.daps.mil. Users may search for decampments using the

ASSIST-Quick Search and, in most cases, download the documents directly via the Internet using standard browser software. Documents not available for downloading from ASSIST can be ordered from the DODSSP using the ASSIST Shopping Wizard, after establishing a DODSSP Customer Account by following the registration procedures or by phoning the DoDSSP Special Assistance Desk at (215) 697-2179 (DSN: 442-2179).Users not having access to the Internet may contact the DODSSP Special Assistance Desk at (215) 697-2179 (DSN: 442-2179 or mail requests to the DODSSP, Bldg. 4/D, 700 Robbins Avenue, Philadelphia, PA 19111-5094. Patterns, Drawings, Deviations Lists, Purchase Descriptions, etc., are not stocked at the DODSSP.

10. Reserved.

11. Reserved.

12. One or more of the items under this acquisition may be subject to an Agreement on Government Procurement approved and implemented in the United States by the Trade Agreements Act of 1979. All offers shall be in the English language and in U.S. dollars. All interested suppliers may submit an offer.

13. The proposed contract is restricted to domestic sources under the authority of FAR 6.302-3. Accordingly, foreign sources, except Canadian sources, are not eligible for award.

14. Reserved.

15. Reserved.

16. Reserved.

17. Reserved.

18. Reserved.

19. Reserved.

20. Reserved.

21. Reserved.

22. The proposed contract action is for supplies or services for which the Government intends to solicit and negotiate with only one source under the authority of FAR 6.302. Interested persons may identify their interest and capability to respond to the requirement or submit proposals. This notice of intent is not a request for competitive proposals. However, all proposals received within forty-five days (thirty days if award is issued under an existing basic ordering agreement) after date of publication of this synopsis, will be considered by the Government. A determination by the Government not to compete with this proposed contract based upon responses to this notice is solely within the discretion of the Government. Information received will normally be considered solely for the purpose of determining whether to conduct a competitive procurement.

23. Award will be made only if the offeror, the product/service or the manufacturer meets qualification requirement at time of award, in accordance with FAR clause 52.209-1 or 52.209.2. The solicitation identifies the office where additional information can be obtained concerning qualification requirements and is cited in each individual solicitation.

24. Architect-Engineering firms which meet the requirements described in this announcement are invited to submit: (1) a Standard Form 254, Architect-Engineer and Related Services Questionnaire, (2) a Standard Form 255, Architect-Engineer and Related Services Questionnaire for Specific Project, when requested, and (3) any requested supplemental data to the procurement office shown. Firms having a current Standard Form 254 on file with the procurement office shown are not required to register this form. Firms desiring to register foe consideration for future projects administered by the procurement office (subject to specific requirements for individual projects) are encouraged to submit annually, a statement of qualifications and per-

formance data, utilizing Standard Form 254, Architect-Engineer and Related Services Questionnaire. Firms responding to this announcement before the closing date will be considered for selection, subject to any limitations indicated with respect to size and geographic location of firm, specialized technical expertise or other requirements listed. Following an initial evaluation of the qualification and performance data submitted, three or more firms that are considered to be the most highly qualified to provide the type of services required, will be chosen for negotiation. Selection of firms for negotiation shall be made through an order of preference based on demonstrated competence and qualifications necessary for the satisfactory performance of the type of professional services required, that include: (1) professional capabilities; (2) specialized experience and technical competence, as required; (3) capacity to accomplish the work in the required time; (4) past performance on contracts with respect to cost control, quality of work, and compliance with performance schedules; (5) geographical location and knowledge of the locality of the project, provided that application of the criterion leaves an appropriate number of qualified firms, given the nature and size of the project; (6) any other special qualification required under this announcement by the contracting activity. In addition to the above qualifications, special qualifications in the Department of Defense include the volume of work previously awarded to the firm by the Department of Defense, with the object of effecting an equitable distribution of Department of Defense architect engineer contracts among qualified architect engineer firms including small and small disadvantaged business firms, and firms that have not had prior Department of Defense contracts.

25. Information submitted should be pertinent and specific in the technical area under consideration, on each of the following qualifications: (1) Experience: An outline of previous projects, specific work previously performed or being performed and any in-house research and development effort; (2) Personnel: Name, professional qualifications and specific experience of scientist, engineers and technical personnel who may be assigned as a principal investigator and/or project officer;

(3) Facilities: Availability and description of special facilities required to perform in the technical areas under consideration. A statement regarding industry security clearance. Any other specific and pertinent information as pertains to this particular area of procurement that would enhance our consideration and evaluation of the information submitted.

26. Based upon market research, the Government is not using the policies contained in Part 12, Acquisition of Commercial Items, in its solicitation for the described supplies or services. However, interested persons may identify to the contracting officer their interest and capability to satisfy the Government's requirement with a commercial item within 15 days of this notice.

27. The proposed contract is set-aside for HUBZone small business concerns. Offers from other than HUBZone small business concerns will not be considered.

28. The proposed contract is set-aside for Very Small Business Concerns (VSB). A VSB is a small business concern whose headquarters is located within the geographic area served by a district designated by SBA; and which, together with its affiliates, has no more than 15 employees and has average annual receipts that do not exceed $1 million. Offers from other than very small business concerns will not be considered.

Bill had familiarized himself with the various numbers even though he didn't try to memorize them. In spite of not memorizing them, Bill found he didn't have to look-up the more popular Numbered Notes used in the type of business he was mostly interested in pursuing. In fact, after doing only a few searches on the FedBizOpps' website, Bill noticed that he could fly through the last three day's filtered notices. It didn't surprise him though because it was kind of part of his plan. That he *expected* it was probably more accurate.

The Numbered Note "8" advised that "The solicitation document contains information that has been designated as 'Militarily Critical Technical

Data' …" Bill checked a few other things and surmised the item(s) most likely required a higher level contract quality system, which Bill inferred as an ISO certification. Whether Bill was right or not at this point was not as important as Bill's decision to filter-out requests that might be wrong for Techno-Systems at this time. It was a poor analogy (in spirit), but Bill had decided to "pick his battles." Plan your work, work your plan. Fail to plan, plan to fail.

Bill was not under any pressure to pursue any and every invitation or request that looked remotely doable. In fact, if Techno-Systems had been desperate for business, it would be even less practical to pursue questionable government business. Bill had "x" amount of time to allocate to prospecting and he could put it to better use than to chase after a tough job. If and when Bill or somebody else had the time, they could refine their searches.

An interesting thought Bill had heard expressed at the PTAC seminar was the way the government may look at the bid you might submit as something you put together entirely on your own. Yes, you were basically just filling in the blanks they provided but, when the bid is received, the government may act like they had never seen it before. The point being, if and when the government signs it, it has become your binding contract. It's important and a bidder can't just gloss over it, sign it and worry about it later. No matter how proficient a bidder becomes at reading requests, it will always behoove them to make absolutely sure they understand what they're reading. The government will consider everything in your bid as what you said you *will* do.

Reading an Invitation for Bid (IFB), a Request for Proposal (RFP) or a Request for Quote (RFQ) can be a daunting task because of the sheer length or the perceived complexity of it. Bill's old employer, way back in B.C. (Before Computer), used to order bid packages by reading a hard copy of Commerce Business Daily, replaced by FedBizOpps, and ordered the bid packages based on a short description of said package. The contract copy was printed out (50 pages not uncommon) and every technical data sheet (prints, again 50 not uncommon) on aperture cards.

An aperture card was like a photographic slide which would then have to be converted to a hard copy print. An expensive proposition for all concerned, bidder and government. Bill's old employer would receive bid packages in the mail every day and some days, if the envelope was too thick, the request was considered too complex and simply thrown away without even opening. A grand waste of money although the government in its zeal to be fair to all potential bidders, felt it incumbent to treat everyone the same way. It was probably the right thing to do at the time.

The number of the solicitation for bid, or just plain "solicitation" said a lot about the origin of the solicitation:

- The first six (possibly less) positions of the number identify the issuing agency or department.

- The next two positions are the last two digits of the fiscal year.

- The single alpha character identifies the type of solicitation:

-     Q=RFQ

-     R= RFP

-     B= IFB

-     P= Purchase Order

-     C= Contract

- The last four numbers are unique to that particular solicitation.

- There was more to it than this but this was just a guideline for general information.

"Presolicitation Notice" might not necessarily mean what you think it might. It could be the only notice issued rather than ultimately being converted to a "Solicitation Notice." Also be aware of the types of notices: "Synopsis, Modification, Amendment, etc." Again, it pays to make a hard copy of the "FBO Vendors Guide" or like information for reference.

Reference. It reminded Bill to check his government dictionary:

Amendment: A change to a solicitation before contract award (also see modification, which occurs after contract award).

Bid: An offer to perform the work described in a contract at a specified cost. A complete and properly signed proposal to do the work. Competition for a job based on lowest cost to do the work. Bids are generally cost specific, based on the cost of labor, materials, profit, and over-head. Bids are normally not negotiated and cannot be changed once accepted by the owner. Bids are time sensitive and are generally good for 30 to 60 days after the bid opening.

Invitation for Bid (IFB): Formal solicitation for offerings, to perform procurements by competitive bids when the specifications describe the requirements of the agency clearly and accurately.

Modification: A change after contract award.

Request for Proposal (RFP): All documents, whether attached or incorporated by reference, utilized for soliciting proposals; the RFP procedure usually requires negotiation with offering party as distinguished from competitive bidding when using an invitation for bids.

Request for Quotation (RFQ): A type of solicitation used typically with small dollar contracts or purchase, but may be used for commercial items up to an agency's prescribed dollar limit.

Responsible Bidder: A business entity that has the capability in all respects to perform fully the contract requirements and whose integrity and reliability will assure good faith performance. Factors considered in evaluating responsibility may include: financial resources, past performance, delivery capability, experience, organization, personnel, technical skills, operations controls, equipment, and facilities.

Set-aside: A contract designated for small or minority bidding only.

Scope of Work: The purpose is to provide bidders with a clear, accurate, and complete description of the work to be performed, including inspection, test and acceptance.

Specification: A description of the technical requirements for a material, product, or service that includes the criteria for determining whether these requirements are met. A specification may describe the performance parameters that a supplier has to meet, or it may provide a complete design disclosure of the work or job to be done. Specifications for service contracts normally take the form of a statement of work.

Statement of Work (SOW): That portion of the contract that clearly and concisely defines requirements of the specific work to be accomplished. Statements of work are individually tailored to consider the period of performance, deliverable items, if any, and the desired degree of performance flexibility. In the case of task order contracts, the SOW for the basic contract only defines the scope of the overall contract in general terms. The SOW for each task order must articulate the specific requirement.

The seminars offered by your PTAC, Bill admitted, were a big help when initially familiarizing oneself with reading and understanding requests. They were excellent at explaining how to read a solicitation and what was extra important, although, of course, it was all important. Bill found he could learn a lot just by the item number.

The National Stock Number (NSN) was the unique 13 digit identification number assigned by the Defense Logistics Agency (DLA) to a given item. It consists of the 4 digit Federal Supply Class/Code (FSC) and the 9 digit National Item Identification Number (NIIN) code.

Format: XXXX-XX-XXX-XXXX (13 digits, all numeric) (NSN)

<u>XX</u>xx-xx-xxx-xxxx = The first two digits are the Federal Supply Group (FSG) that identifies a general group of related items.

<u>XXXX</u>-xx-xxx-xxxx = The first four digits are the FSC that identifies a specific sub grouping of items.

xxxx-<u>XX</u>-xxx-xxxx = The fifth and sixth digits identifies the country of manufacture: 00 = United States

    01 = United States
    12 = Germany
    14 = France
    15 = Italy

99 = United Kingdom

Etc.

xxxx-xx-<u>XXX-XXXX</u> = The seventh through thirteenth digits are sequentially assigned by computer at the Defense Logistics Information Service (DLIS) in Battle Creek, MI where the NSN database is located. These numbers are collectively known as the NIIN and are unique to that particular item.

Bill could see the value of understanding the item numbers when you were looking for opportunities and preferred to stay within supply groups. Or, if he came across an item that looked familiar, he could probably determine how the item could possibly be used. And if he kept his own spreadsheet of item's histories and drawings, he could group the item numbers accordingly.

Back to his request, Bill had second thoughts about the Numbered Note 8, and asked Mary to send Kevin in if she could see him out there. Bill heard him talking a little earlier and would ask Kevin's opinion if was convenient for Kevin.

"Hi Bill," said Kevin. "What's up?"

Bill explained his logic and Kevin concurred.

Bill remembered something else and asked if the detective, Meadows, had been talking to anyone from Techno-Systems.

"Not that I know of," replied Kevin.

Bill thanked him and got back to the business at hand.

Kevin wondered what the last part was all about. He knew that he himself didn't have anything to worry about from the police but sometimes his brother Jeremy gave him pause for thought. While it was true that Jeremy didn't get outwardly excited about much of anything, a deeper part of him didn't drop things so easily. Oh yes, Jeremy could be still percolating years after a Jeremy perceived insult occurred.

The only indication of how serious the perceived situation was would be the length of time from the incident occurring and Jeremy saying, "Okay." No one really knew if that meant Jeremy accepted the truth of what occurred or he was making a mental note to finish something later.

The way that people talked was usually the way they thought. For instance, if someone never finished a sentence, stopping after saying something like "but," that's as far as their mind probably got. Whatever else Jeremy may have thought after saying okay probably meant Jeremy's mind was at ease, for now.

Jeremy was a "don't get mad, get even" kind of guy, even though he would rarely get even with anyone. The thought of getting even would tide him over until the heat of the moment passed. All of that would have made sense if that was as far as Jeremy took it. And it may well have been as far as it would go but, depending on the depth of the perceived issue, Jeremy consoled himself that someone could die.

Really die. Heavy thought but Jeremy had a list of everyone who had, in his opinion, done him really dirty. Over the years, Jeremy had up to seven names on the list though never more than three at a time and the odds were high that the last name on the list would be scratched-off as well. Jeremy didn't even know other than he had actually planned (in his mind) how to make him disappear once. Jeremy was probably dead serious.

Kevin knew all this because Jeremy had admitted an intolerance for being screwed. Kevin also understood a person's perception. To that particular person, that perception was fact. This knowledge had served Kevin well over the years when trying to analyze another person's thought process. It was unlikely that Denny Bell was on Jeremy's "hit list" but, you never know. Better to keep it to himself so not to open a can of worms for nothing.

While Kevin was thinking about Jeremy's possible involvement, Bill was thinking about Donny, the company rabble-rouser wherever he worked. If anyone even cared enough to ask him, Donny would have said Patti was the likely suspect. Patti couldn't help but think that Bill seemed really happy the way it was turning out. Maybe deep down inside, Patti just liked the idea of a "White Knight" making wrong right or somehow defending her honor. General consensus at the cop shop was the duo of Patti and Bill, primarily because they were historically the most likely perpetrators, statistically speaking. Detective Meadows didn't care what anyone thought as long as it favored whatever he was thinking at the time to clear his case.

9

Technical Data

Sometimes the description in the solicitation was enough to determine what to quote. If an item was identified as commercial or an equivalent that might be enough unless reverse engineering was necessary. If the item was to be manufactured to a specification, the odds were high that a drawing or print was needed. The first thing that the many job shops vying for government business usually wanted was a print and, for Bill's type of product, a set of prints was also paramount.

If a picture was worth a thousand words, not using a print to describe a service, instead of a product, made Bill wonder how many words *that* took. The government was procuring outside services at an increasing rate to replace those services deemed too costly for the government to continue providing. Bill saw tons of requests in the FBO when he checked for Techno-System and couldn't help but wonder if there could be an opportunity for offering some sort of service, but, first things first.

In Bill's short experience in searching for items to quote on, the most glaring problem was a print, or rather, lack of one, with a solicitation. This was an issue for Bill because since he was open to considering a variety of manufactured items, he looked at a diverse variety of requests. The PTAC had advised him to go on to the next request if prints were unavailable although Bill didn't think it was right to advertise for something that, without drawings for new bidders, just wasted everyone's time. If the buying office was simply going through the motions to pretend to satisfy a mandate, then the system was broken.

Bill supposed that *not* making prints available could be used as a filter to minimize the number of bidders responding a particular request. The FBO was better about it than some of the agency or location sites advertising their own requests. In those cases, the only opportunity was for a previous supplier to supply the item again. At one popular site, Bill noticed hundreds of advertised needs without drawings available. The ray of hope that he could get from that was the thought of it having to get better. If and when reform came, at least Bill would be ready.

The "local" PTAC had a worthwhile program for assisting small businesses locate some of the drawings not available with the requests. One of the specialists had actually been collecting drawings, when available, on a computer for years. If any of their clients would call on a part number which was saved, they could get drawings and specs in short order.

Most of the PTACs offered technical assistance of prints and data sheets at little or no cost to the bidder. If the data is so common that it's only referenced, they can provide that information as well. The SBA representative, Rosemary Haberberg, suggested contacting them for some data although she said that the SBA usually defers to the PTAC for any technical data. Along with specific information, the PTAC had access to all sorts of general information for the prospective bidder. Some of the staff were specialized in certain areas, giving them a high level of expertise in their particular disciplines.

Ever since Patti had registered Techno-Systems in the CCR data base, Bill had been receiving emails every week from private firms offering their "custom services." Most were for bidding services though a few offered complete bid packages, hard copies of the contract, drawings, data sheets, etc., for a fee, of course. The fee seemed high but a lot of work could go into converting everything to hard copy or even compiling all of the data in a printer-friendly format for the bidder. Bill knew "nothing is free" (a PTAC was paid by taxpayers), "you get what you pay for" and the ever popular "buyer beware" all applied.

The best long term solution for a serious government contractor was to build their own library of technical data. The amount of variety in a bidder's interest would determine the size of the library needed although most would be quite sizeable. Files could be entered and saved by item numbers as they were available. Only those items or series of items pertaining to the bidder's interests would be kept for reference as often as the request was repeated. While it might seem like a huge project, if it was done on a regular basis and in a timely fashion, it was doable Bill thought.

A spreadsheet on a computer or in hard copy would avoid duplication and be easy to reference. Bill preferred, as usual, a hard copy of the listings while keeping the detail on his computer and a backup disc. The specifications and standards germane to Techno-Systems' type of work were also saved and referenced the same way.

Bill loved the "information highway" on his computer and believed that all roads led to whatever he entered for search criteria. If he tried a few variations on a common theme, Bill knew that he could locate the most current and detailed information on any subject imaginable. This time he entered "federal government specifications" and came-up with a link to a site called "Acquisition Central" with even more specific links.

FedTeDS (Federal Technical Data Solutions) is a web application designed to safeguard acquisition related information while enabling the distribution and dissemination, or dispersal, of "Sensitive But Unclassified (SBU) information to vendors. Bill visited the site of a Press Release:

Washington D.C.—The need for a secure online dissemination tool arose from the requirement that all Federal Agencies must provide on-line material to commercial vendors, as outlined in the Freedom of Information Act (FoIA). Currently, over 90 Federal Agencies are disseminating SBU acquisition materials during the solicitation phase of procurement via the Internet. This material includes information related to operations, systems, structures, individuals and services essential to the security and management of a facility, including tele-communications, electrical power, building facility structural layout, gas and oil storage/transportation, water supply, emergency services, and the continuity of operations. Much of this information could pose a possible threat to national security if made public.

FedTeDS.gov empowers Federal Agencies to embrace safeguarding requirements for accessing critical information available on the Internet.

FedTeDS specifically addresses the following:

- Improves the efficiency, credibility, and effectiveness of the acquisition and logistics support process by streamlining the Federal procurement process.

- Allows for real time vendor access to SBU acquisition material, saving government agencies valuable time and dollars.

- Establishes a physical firewall between the Federal government and its public customers providing additional security without decreasing vendor satisfaction.

- Utilizes existing Department of Defense(DoD) databases to validate a user's access to export controlled data.

Interesting, thought Bill, how the federal government disseminates what they want you to know about dissemination. Patti had already registered with FedTeDS since she had taken care of the CCR registration and knew the MPIN (Marketing Partner Identification Number) issued upon CCR completion. She had also needed their DUNS number or CAGE Code, telephone number and email address.

So, FedTeDS registration was a done deal although Bill decided to have Patti register Techno-System and his personal name for certification under the U.S./Canada Joint Certification Program. Bill thought back to the solicitations he had passed over because of the Numbered Note 8 on "Militarily Critical Technical Data" only businesses being eligible. It really wasn't as difficult as he thought to be certified by the JCP other than completing and submitting a "DD Form 2345." The DLIS (Defense Logistics Information Service) assigns and maintains the certification numbers at no charge although it was necessary to change the password periodically. Yes, definitely a duty to be assigned to his increasingly important ally, Patti.

Bill had been advised by the PTAC of a few other websites for drawings when attending their basic seminar. The buying centers in Philadelphia, Richmond and Columbus all had their own websites and same with the Army and Navy, but responsibility seemed a little hazy. At the time, a transition to a more single source was in the works though Bill depended primarily on the solicitation posting for direction on an individual basis. He had visited all of the websites suggested to build-up his basic background knowledge but so far the FBO had everything he needed. As Bill expanded his prospecting, his technical sources could change as well.

Kevin had been shown a CD that his fellow inspector at another company had received from the government. He told Kevin that their company had gotten the CD too late for them to quote but wouldn't let Kevin take it back to Bill because it could violate something or other. Kevin supposed that was true though he thought Bill would have been amazed at all of the information on the disc. It must be the computer equivalent of boilerplate on a printed solicitation only easier for the buyer to add to a CD. Every time his friend opened another file, it seemed to lead to another set of files. "Incredible," Kevin had told Bill at the time.

Bill was getting more effective and efficient at processing government information while Kevin, being new to such a data overload, would rightly feel the need to read every file. Bill knew what files he could gloss over in the reviewing a solicitation stage and go back to if he decided to actually quote on the job. He was looking forward to his first CD to see for himself because of the way Kevin had described it. Apparently, the more solicitations you process, the more extraneous technical material you can identify as "boilerplate," and initially gloss over it. Ultimately though, if Bill decided to quote on a solicitation, he planned on reading every word until he was totally confident on what he was quoting on and before signing an offer.

10

Shipping Requirements

Bill had heard horror stories about successful bidders winning a contract only to find out they had bid the packaging requirements too low. The government has precise needs to ensure the protection of the item during shipping, storage and distribution because of the extreme variables the item may be subjected to before being used. Identification has become a huge factor to the government in determining what they may have or may need. Every type of packing, packaging and marking is, of course, stated by a rather lengthy specification.

During Bill's search for shipping specifications, he came across a history of how different methods had to be addressed because of the World Wars being fought in such diverse conditions. From the North Pole to the South Pole and every condition experienced in-between, the product had to be maintained like new until it was needed. The history was actually kind of interesting, at least as much as Bill had time to read. It gave him a new appreciation of why packing and packaging methods were so important.

Identification of what the government had on hand led to what the government needed and when they needed it. The amount of inventory the government needed to conduct regular day-to-day business plus whatever else they might be involved with at any given time was mind-boggling. Computers must have seemed like a Godsend when they were first utilized to control the huge and scattered inventory.

Bill remembered back when bar-coding was first specified by the government for items shipped by his previous employer. It seemed pretty exotic at the time but now even Techno-Systems used it for some of their commercial accounts. In fact, Techno-Systems printed many of the strips they used on their own economical printer and affordable software. He supposed every new requirement by the government was probably met with some reluctance by their vendors.

The new requirement for Radio Frequency Identification (RFID) now seemed exotic to Bill although he was sure if the government said it must be used, the sheer quantity of products affected would make it popular. Popularity led to competition which led to lower pricing on the technology and easier availability to small businesses. Based on that premise, Bill decided not to worry too much about it, other than making sure its cost was covered in any quotes.

Bill had assigned Bill Sexton to look into the packaging and shipping requirement and he had come back to Bill after a week or so and announced that "it was all covered." Bill was skeptical until Bill S. told him he had "given up trying to figure it out by himself" and "had called in the 'professionals' for a solution."

The "professionals" turned out to a packaging and shipping contractor, in a city only 90 miles from Techno-Systems. They specialized in anything government, was one of two packaging contractors Bill S. had researched and they had worked with a friend of his in the past. Both contractors had excellent references though so Bill S. would have a back-up source if needed.

"Are they comprehensive enough for small parts to a whole machine?" asked Bill N.

"Oh yeah. They're able to actually administer complete contracts, provide all labels and bar-coding, radio frequency I.D., complete forms, help with computer transactions, everything. You name it, they can do it."

"Well, you're getting off kind of easy for right now but if this takes off, I'd probably like to bring it in house," said Bill N.

"No problemo, Mr. Bill," answered Bill S.

Deep down inside, Bill N. was glad that he didn't have to worry about the details of meeting governmental packaging and shipping requirements, only the cost. Techno-System's competitors would have the same cost unless they had provisions to do it all in-house, and even then the overall cost would be a factor for them as well.

Bill had heard of a screw machine house that got a nice contract at a decent profit only to find out the packaging cost more than the part. The supplier got out of the deal because of the good graces of the Contracting Officer. The CO could have held the screw machine company accountable and it would have been a very grim experience for them. Each tiny part had to be chemically protected, in its own sealed bag and labeled accordingly. The vendor was used to shipping in bulk and their idea of how much the packaging would cost was a joke compared to reality.

No doubt about it. Bill would defer to the experts for the time being.

11

Best Price

Detective Craig Meadows and his new partner, Detective Albert Kahler, were at Techno-Systems on an apparent mission later that day. Bill thought it was a mission because Meadows didn't bother asking Mary if he was in, instead the detective walked up to Bill's open office door and announced: "It wasn't suicide. Was it?"

Bill did a double take and looked at the new guy behind Meadows.

"Hello, I'm Detective Al Kahler. I'm assigned to work with Detective Meadows."

Meadows: "Nelson, you and Patti Bell have a problem."

Kahler: "Mr. Nelson, new evidence has come to light. A third party has come forward with allegations of an arrangement between you and Mrs. Bell. It may be nothing but Detective Meadows feels it to be a major development."

Bill: "I have no idea what you're talking about."

Meadows: "Call Patti Bell in here. Now."

Kahler: "Is Mrs. Bell available?"

Bill: "Can you tell me who said what?"

Meadows: "The answer is, I don't know. I know, but I won't say."

Kahler: "It was one of Mr. Bell's ex-employees."

Bill: "Is the ex-employee working here now?"

Meadows: "No, but I'm not going to tell you."

Bill, looking only slightly relieved asked, "was it Donny? He's the only old employee I didn't want back."

Kahler: "Thanks, Craig."

Meadows: "It doesn't matter. It will come out pretty quick anyway." To Bill: "You and Patti Bell are under arrest for the murder of Dennis Bell!"

Kahler: "Slow down, Craig. For one thing, Mrs. Bell has to be here to be put under arrest and, besides, we agreed to just talk to them today." To Bill: "Detective Meadows is perhaps premature but we would like to visit with you and Mrs. Bell separately now and maybe we can clear this up here rather than the station."

Bill: "I understand. For your information, Patti isn't here right now. Maybe back in a few minutes. Oh, there she is."

They visited with both Bill and Patti after Meadows calmed down. In an aside with Bill, Detective Kahler confided that his partner was now actually his junior partner and was under tremendous pressure to solve this case. His superiors had never been happy with the suicide theory earlier and discovered that most of Detective Meadow's cases were explained away by whatever convenient answer he could fabricate. After almost two hours of questioning Bill and Patti, the two detectives left to visit with the perpetually disgruntled former employee again.

"Well, that was weird," said Bill when he was alone with Patti.

"Sure was. Is Donny liable for saying lies about us?"

"Probably not, but the police won't be too happy with him if they can prove he lied. "He'll figure out some way to say it was just what he understood, I suppose."

"I suppose it didn't help when you bought Systems-Plus and we started dating so soon after Denny's death, but we were divorced. It actually makes me feel better than I did for not inviting him back. Kind of confirms that he's a jerk. Let him be someone else's problem. Hey, while you're in here, I'm ready to work out a price on our first quote to Uncle Sam."

Bill really didn't need Patti to help him calculate a price although she had become his confidante on major decisions concerning Techno-System. Mostly because they were still discussing marriage without a prenuptial, everything 50/50, right down the middle. Patti had actually helped Bill to buy-out Systems-Plus from the money Bill had given her for Techno-System. Plus, and maybe this was a factor in the police so ready to believe Donny, Patti had also received an insurance settlement on Denny's death. In fact, she now had a higher net worth than Bill. Miz GotBucks.

The first action Bill had taken upon finding the solicitation he was working on was to call his PTAC to check on the item's pricing history. They came back to him almost immediately with a complete history including more information than Bill thought possible. That was easy enough. Not all histories were so easy to find although the PTAC and the SBA had offered their assistance and Bill had resolved to work with them as much as possible.

Some of the solicitations offered information, usually through a link to a central location for technical data or more directly through the agency advertising the solicitation. Some of the larger buying centers would show if additional information was available from them. And, of course, there were a glut of private companies offering their services. The PTAC Bill worked with used a private service which was probably the Cadillac of such services although with their high demand, they could justify the expense.

Bill was contacted by a private service with very competitive rates shortly after registering in the CCR. For a nominal fee, they offered incumbent pricing and payment history, a variety of searching tools, info on ordering FoIA or FOIA (Freedom of Information Act) records, and many other helpful services. Bill was skeptical over the unusually fair subscription fee but would check it out down the road. Private service companies assisting contracting wannabes and established contractors seemed to be popping-up all over. Bill took it as a sign of growing opportunities.

Under the FoIA (Freedom of Information Act), all, in theory, federal agencies were generally required to disclose records requested in writing by any person. However, agencies may withhold information pursuant to nine exemptions and three exclusions contained in the statute. The FoIA applies only to federal agencies and does not create a right of access to records held by Congress, the courts, or by state or local government agencies. Each state has its own public access laws that should be consulted for access to state and local records. Bill was primarily interested in only federal records pertaining to past procurement information.

Each federal agency is responsible for meeting its FoIA responsibilities for its own records. A list of *Principal FoIA Contacts At Federal Agencies* is available over the internet although contacting a PTAC or the SBA could prove helpful, certainly more responsive, and thus, more effective. Bill knew that the government was in a particular state of flux over releasing information at the present time. He decided to treat each one on an individual basis for now and research the FoIA more in-depth when he had more time.

The system as Bill understood it had been established by an act of Congress in 1979 in an attempt to provide a clear window into the sometimes murky world of federal contracting although there had been recent changes. Much of the collection, distribution and even the database itself had turned over to a private contractor by the GSA and may not be subject to the FoIA. If this situation stands, the American Public will lose an important tool to monitor and research data. Bill had read a blog to the effect that it could change so he would keep an open mind in case it affected him in the future.

Having access to procurement histories was one of the primary differences in pursuing government business versus commercial business. Some of Techno-Systems' commercial customers would hint at past pricing but none were required to disclose anything. If Techno-Systems secured a contract, the price they had quoted would then be used by their competitors. Bill was aware of this yet confident if they got the contract once, and if the business was profitable, and Techno-Systems had a good past performance history, they could do it again.

Bill had learned that pricing wasn't everything in capturing a government contract though. The government applied "weight factors" in determining how and where they would award contracts. SBA set-asides carried weight. Past performance carried weight. A Contract Officer's personal preferences carried weight. Whatever the factor might be, the government would weigh it all and the scale would tip in favor of the successful bidder.

For some types of bidders, a marketing strategy was more important than the lowest price. Many businesses focus on driving sales leads and figuring out pricing instead of formulating a government marketing strategy.

The government buyers are like most commercial buyers in that overall *value* is more important than price. It definitely takes a plan.

For some suppliers, becoming a GSA (General Services Administration) Schedule contractor is the way to go. The FSS (Federal Supply Service) is the branch of GSA that has responsibilities in procurement and provides federal customers with the products, services and programs they require for meeting their general needs. Almost anything imaginable that the government uses or does while conducting business can be procured, or probably will be someday, through the GSA process.

Getting an FSS contract doesn't mean you've actually sold anything yet and, in itself, does not guarantee any business, but it does mean you're an approved government seller. A "pre-approved" seller to which other government agencies can place orders with for nearly any kind of business product or service. You still have to sell or market what you're offering.

Billions of dollars are spent each year on products and services for the various agencies and the GSA is responsible for ensuring the best quality and value for their federal customers. The federal customers are the various agencies that use a "catalog" comprised of commercial products and services available, already pre-approved and pre-negotiated for the best value. The GSA Schedule is the vehicle to the catalog and is the contract for such products and services.

To become a GSA Schedule contractor, a vendor must first submit an offer, applicable to the GSA Schedule solicitation. The GSA awards contracts to responsible companies that offer commercial items or services falling within the generic descriptions in the GSA solicitation. The Contracting Officers determine whether prices are fair and reasonable by comparing the prices and discounts quoted in the solicitation with prices and discounts offered to the bidder's commercial or best customers. This negotiation objective is commonly known as "most favored customer" pricing. The government essentially is seeking the supplier's best pricing.

A new program, the Multiple Award Schedule Express Program, in the works hopes to speedup the cumbersome GSA listing process by streamlining it. The current average time (optimistic) of 120 days will be improved to 30 days (target).

As in any success in selling to the government, it also makes a statement to a supplier's commercial customers that the supplier can run with the big dogs. They are a cut above their competitors in the marketplace. They are focused and organized enough to be a supplier to the biggest customer in the world and those attributes carry over to their commercial customers as well. Bill made a mental note to check out the GSA Schedules in the future because such schedules may well be the way of the future.

Bill got back to the project at hand, the pricing on the solicitation he was working on. He had a check list of considerations:

- pricing history—done, Bill

- special requirements—quality proof cost, Kevin—packaging cost, Bill S.

- manufacturing costs—Jeremy & Bill

- profit—Bill & Patti

There were other considerations although Bill wanted to delegate as much as practical as quickly as possible. A team of competent people responsible for the areas they knew best. Techno-Systems was not a democracy so, ultimately, Bill was the last word, but he liked the philosophy that "all of us are smarter than any one of us."

Three days later, on a date and time agreed upon by the individual teammates in advance, they all got together and hashed out everything except the profit aspect. That was for Bill even though Patti would be included to double-check his calculations. Patti was also responsible for re-reading the contract and filling in the blanks. Bill would sign it, if it was a hard copy.

Bill had heard another interesting philosophy: "If it doesn't make dollars, it doesn't make cents." It was an old sales adage that he'd also seen as "sense" instead of "cents." Either way, Bill's initial plan did not call for selling at a loss or even trading dollars for a foot in the door. He wanted a little cushion for any unforeseen expenses incurred. Bill knew some manufacturers might lowball but it wasn't for him.

The price he quoted would be very competitive and moderately profitable. A new supplier had to get the Contracting Officer's attention but it probably wouldn't be by the lowest price unless he could actually produce the product the most efficiently. It would appear that only long established and sort of "traditional" suppliers didn't worry about price. The "no-bid" contracts Bill read about in the newspapers seemed to be awarded to the super primes everyone was familiar with but not new aspiring contractors.

There was a rumbling that reform might come to government procurement in the near future because of a few scandals Bill had also read about in the newspaper. If and when it came, Techno-Systems would be ready. Under the system years ago, a lot of what the government procured was manufactured to perhaps overly rigid specifications. The classic example was the legendary $300 hammer that probably cost that much to make with the certification required on every one of its features. The oft quoted $700 toilet seat was actually quite complicated and was used on an expensive bomber. Still, with relaxed specifications considering what it was used for or an effort to standardize somehow, it might have been made more cost efficient.

A concerted effort to convert more of the products and services to more commercial specs was being implemented by the government whenever practical. This practice coincided with the GSA being utilized more often with schedule contracts.

Bill had read about the DoD published guidelines for what was a typical profit for a qualified supplier. At first Bill wasn't sure of what he was reading; that the government would have the audacity and was as fiscally responsible as to tell their vendors how to do it? The television news last week had said that "the U.S. Government was overpaying on over half of what they bought," and this was from their own accounting office. Companies like Techno-Systems had to jump through hoops to even be considered as a supplier and, in Bill's opinion, would save them money, while the government was overpaying other companies?

A confusing contradiction but Bill knew that "the tail doesn't wag the dog" and that if he wanted to sell to the government, he'd have to play by their rules. It was like when Bill was just a kid and another kid would have the only ball, and if you wanted to play ball, it had to be by the other kid's rules. Bill didn't think it was fair but made another mental note to ask the SBA or PTAC about it, for his own edification. But, as usual in life, Bill could only control his immediate situation.

Bill was happy with the price he and his team had calculated on this particular solicitation because it had a satisfactory profit margin built in albeit less margin than usual for commercial. He wouldn't necessarily buy business but he wanted to draw blood on his first quote. It did have to be low enough to get the Contracting Officer's attention though and give Techno-Systems an opportunity to prove their worthiness.

One more step completed.

12

Proposal Writing

Bill found all sorts of websites with helpful hints on submitting proposals to the federal government, usually at some cost to the bidder. He found every imaginable tool: from free to pricey to templates to edit to a service offering to do everything for him. But first, Bill had to get it clear in his mind of what the proposal actually was. He was currently working on a form to fill out and submit either electronically or in hard copy, although it seemed that everything he read suggested having to submit an involved written proposal, like a mini-book, at this stage of the process.

Bill had attended the worthwhile seminar a number of months ago on the basics of government contracting with a vow to attend their more specific seminar on proposal writing when he had time. Bill hadn't known that an opportunity would present itself before the next seminar. He emailed the PTAC and briefly explained the situation and received a reply within the hour. Their suggestion was to complete the form to the best of his ability and to email, mail or bring in the Solicitation/Contract to them for review. It was important to do all this ASAP to make sure the necessary data was reviewed, corrected if needed and submitted to the Contracting Officer in time.

Fair enough, thought Bill. He had decided months ago to do as much research himself as practical to get the job done right without over-studying the issues. There were a variety of possible types of bids and different methods to submit them to the contracting office. Even the impending seminar on proposal writing was intended, in Bill's mind at least, to give him an awareness of what was to be done and some of the obvious pitfalls to avoid, but not to make him an expert.

The experts at the PTAC and SBA would help him as long as he didn't expect them to do all of the work. After he took any particular quote or whatever as far as he could, they could give him direction and/or verify that his efforts were correct. Bill had printed out and compiled a three-ring binder of every manual or guide offered over the internet by the various government agencies, then tabbed the content. The info from SBA and PTAC was included along with the outline of the seminar he had attended. This resource could be added to, updated and referred to whenever necessary. Bill would also verify with the PTAC what he understood before making any important commitments until he was totally confident in his own expertise.

Bill's plan was to research any particular issue in depth only after he had surmised that it was germane to the project. That way he probably wouldn't be wasting his time with any more details than necessary for the job at hand. Bill had surrounded himself like-thinkers who would become experts in their own right on any subject they were involved with, sort of like osmosis.

The PTAC had a sample of the form Bill had to submit with the absolutely mandatory data to be completed highlighted. There were a few other aids for Bill which would be included in the package being snail-mailed to Techno-Systems. He was pleased to utilize their services as much as necessary to ensure that his first couple of submittals were accurate.

A newly acquired skill was the speed of reviewing quotes which was something Bill was to hone in the coming months. It was simple. The more often you did something, the faster each time it could be done. Not only faster but even more effectively. This was in large part to the increased level of confidence gained with experience. This increase in personal and company-wide confidence would be evidenced time and time again as federal contracting became a bigger part of Techno-Systems' business.

Bill had delegated Patti as the "final proposal writer/form filler outer person" in the company. It was an obviously informal title he had given her because she was not only was the best writer, she was maybe the most accurate writer. Her writing skills wouldn't be fully utilized on this quote although on any correspondence, misspelled words would be considered sloppy. If you don't bother to spell everything correctly, it might be inferred that your quality could be sloppy too. Sloppiness does not reflect well on the credibility of what you're telling them you can and will do. This particular contract was perfect for their first venture into the government market because it was fairly straightforward.

The PTAC had advised Bill that in 90 percent of the smaller contracts for common products or services would be evaluated strictly and quickly on price, terms and delivery. On those types of cases, it's simply a matter of filling in the price and delivery and sending it back in, although Techno-Systems' quote was a little more involved.

Another part of Bill's plan was to try and work with the same agencies as much as possible to understand better how they operate. He wanted to learn the ins and outs of a couple of agency markets before tackling the others. From what Bill had gleaned from reading the solicitations, there seemed to be a commonality of requirements from specific agencies and he could use that to increase his effectiveness in prospecting. Then as he expanded his horizons, he'd be more confident in his work, his accuracy of understanding and his efficiency.

There was a website just for forms and Patti had compiled copies of the more popular ones for Bill to do a rough draft and then Patti to do the final submittal. Bill had decided to send Patti to the next PTAC seminar on proposal writing and if he would be available, he'd attend too. Kind of a cheap date.

Bill was the primary Salesperson for Techno-Systems but he was planning on hiring a full-time Salesperson or Sales Manager sometime in the future. He wanted to be able to spend more time with the girls than every other weekend. Most companies the size of Techno-Systems had a sales department but Techno-Systems had evolved so far without one. They were growing at a comfortable rate now and the absorbing of Systems-Plus was justifying the addition.

Bill had information on more complex negotiated proposals, thanks to his best source, the internet. He had already passed the info to Patti though he had kept copies for himself. One sheet was a list supposedly written by a group of government Contract Officers explaining they wanted in a proposal:

- Give us exactly what we asked for in the RFP, no more or no less.

- Avoid sales pitches without substantiation.

- Keep it short, concise, lucid and to the point.

- Present a practical, no-nonsense solution that mets our requirements precisely and tell us how your solution will benefit us.

- Discuss the risk involved with your solution and how you plan to mitigate it.

- Don't throw in boilerplate for the sake of impressing the evaluators.

- Tell us exactly who will staff the contract and provide a pertinent resume for each proposed key staff. Don't waffle on whether the proposed staff member is actually available and that you are committed to providing the person.

- Tell us your pertinent qualifications but don't overdo it with experience descriptions that repeat themselves.

- Tailor everything you write to the request. All proposal content should be request specific including resumes and organization experience.

- Say it with tightly organized content presented in simple, declarative sentences.

- Evaluators state that the two major sins of proposal writing are use of off-the-shelf boilerplate and presentation of extraneous, unwanted material.

- Make our job easier and write to the evaluation criteria. Focus on solving our requirements as stated in the request and the risks and benefits of your solution.

- The approach that evaluators prefer is called defensive proposal writing or defending your position as a potential contractor.

- Avoid too much industry specific jargon as it may be unfamiliar to the evaluator.

Good stuff to know directly from the people who know. The defensive proposal writing does not mean being apologetic. Always think and write positively without seeming to apologize for any weaknesses you might think you have. You are selling your abilities and must instill confidence to the reader that you will be able to perform when awarded the contract. Bill had already advised Patti to be completely honest, factual and as confident as possible without overly bragging.

Bill also had copies of the proposal outline, or guideline, explaining what information a typical proposal would contain and a fairly standard format to use. However, this information was readily available from a number of websites and Patti could follow them if and when they might have to write a formal proposal. Bill felt good about having Patti to do the detail work and she felt good about having the skills to contribute.

As Bill reflected on possible RFP's to be addressed in the future, he considered the statement he had heard at the basic contracting seminar. One of the attendees had read that replying to an RFP (Request for Proposal) was probably a waste of time and effort. Bill recalled this situation from his visit with the SBA and offered his understanding that in many cases, the buyer was only going through the motions to satisfy a "multiple quote required" requirement. That the supplier had already been chosen and any additional proposals in reply to the requesting agency was for reference only. If that was true, a sincere but naïve bidder could waste a lot of time for the honor of justifying another successful bidder's quote. Again, if true, it was a horribly unfair practice. Bill had already decided to ask the PTAC before responding to any RFP's, but the reminder didn't hurt.

Another rumor involving proposals that Bill asked Patti to check-out before returning theirs was to not use staples. In bidding legend, a single staple could earn your bid a one way ticket to the wastebasket with some Contracting Officers. Talk about horribly unfair. All of that work, casually thrown in the waste basket when there wasn't even anything in writing to warn about this unforgivable sin.

It might not really be true and Bill might not have believed it except for the arrogance exhibited by some in various levels of government. Not everyone in the government appreciated the work invested with submitting offers to them it seemed to Bill, but then it was also understandable how jaded a CO could get after a few years of reviewing submittals.

At any rate, no staples without clearing it first with the PTAC. Bill started to peck in an email to Patti to be careful with the stapler when he thought he heard an unfamiliar voice in the lobby. Shortly after that, Mary knocked softly on his open door frame.

"Mr. Nelson, Detective Kahler is here to see you," she announced. Bill just nodded and she smiled at Bill and then at Kahler before going back to her desk.

"Mr., ah Detective Kahler. How may I help you?" asked Bill. Kahler was alone this time.

"Mr. Nelson," said the detective extending his hand, "sorry for just dropping by. I have some new developments on the case and a few questions." Kahler sat down in the chair after Bill gestured to it.

"Detective Meadows is on an indefinite paid suspension, pending review of some of his cases. Quite a few actually, of which Mr. Bell's has been reopened."

"What happened?" asked Bill.

"The Dennis Bell solution was just too convenient and way too unlikely to have been settled the way it was: suicide. But we're maxed out in the Homicide Department. People upstairs are hoping beyond reality for cases to be cleared and Detective Meadows found a way to manipulate, or abuse, the system ... allegedly. Usually, pressure from relatives or friends keeps the investigations real, but this was just an unlikely combination of an imaginative person put in charge, and not many people who cared about Mr. Bell."

"So, where do we stand now?" asked Bill.

"I'm going over the reports and re-interviewing some people again. So far, nothing's jumping out though."

"How does it affect me, or my company?" asked Bill.

"We're not sure yet, but I'm still trying to get on top of what we already have and what we'll need. I do have a few more questions questions for you and Mrs. Bell. Also a couple of employees from both companies, which I understand are both yours now."

Detective Kahler spent a few hours at Techno-Systems but didn't say anything, one way or the other, before leaving. Bill hadn't had time to talk to Patti yet. He felt like he was in good shape anyway.

Getting ready to do business with the federal government was forcing Techno-Systems to do more things, hopefully more *right* things. Positive things. Positive changes that would be beneficial to their overall growth in the industry, government and commercial business, and in maintaining the effectiveness and profitability of that growth. A pretty good move so far, thought Bill, but it was just starting and if, for some reason, Bill decided not to pursue additional government business in the future, he wouldn't be out anything. The exercise alone was good for the company.

And, even if they didn't pursue more government business *or* the exercise hadn't been good for the company, Bill's love life had never been better. Of course, Bill would never suggest that anyone else should go after federal government business because it would improve their love life although, indirectly, it had for him. Bill remembered Denny saying once that if you tried to sell to the government, you'd end up getting screwed.

13

Review/Submit

Patti was looking extra attractive today and she knew it, or she thought it was at least one of the reasons so many people seemed to be staring at her. Patti wasn't vain but she was at an age where she enjoyed attention to her looks, besides the biological clock business always ticking. Attractive meant more than outside appearances to Patti. It meant that her whole person attracted people to seek her out for pleasantries.

It didn't hurt that her whole person was wrapped in really tight clothing today. And if Patti had evaluated the sources of all the staring, there would have been a much higher ratio of the opposite sex doing the staring. The only person completely indifferent to the provocative styling was Bambi, who was so attractive that she actually tried to dress down at the office. Perfectly good men, like Kevin, turned lecherous around her.

Bill had earlier asked Bambi into his office, to request that she tone down her usual dress during regular workdays at Techno-Systems. Even before that, Bill had suggested to everyone in a memo to dress a little more professional while at work. Bambi took this to mean wear a dress in the office and Bill didn't say anything else about it, at least not to Bambi, until Patti came back. Bambi was innocent and really didn't care what others thought though she was also pretty smart and knew it wasn't coincidence that Bill would mention it only after Patti had returned.

Patti had everything she could think of to submit the bid, especially time enough to do it right. Bill and she had worked out a time schedule of the different events necessary so that each step would be completed by a specific date to lead into the next step. Scheduling projects was not unlike scheduling production in that you had to stay on top of each part of the process. Bill had shared a theory with Patti about how earlier process steps missed would accumulate near the end of a scheduled process. He called it compression.

Bill also related an actual story to show how it worked. When he was in the military too many years ago, his Army Company, Company "B", in Basic Training had to go on long marches. For some reason they were called "forced marches" as though everything else they had to do in Basic was not forced. It was not uncommon to be spread out a single file of soldiers up to a hundred soldiers long. The idea was to keep a distance of ten-feet between each soldier.

If every soldier marched at exactly the same rate of speed, the distance between soldiers was easy to maintain. If the second soldier in line let the gap extend to eleven-feet and then jumped ahead one-foot to catch up, not a problem, right? It would be if the third soldier didn't react immediately and had to jump ahead two-feet to catch up. If it was multiplied by a few more soldiers, the following soldiers would have to run to keep-up with the leader of the whole shebang, who was just walking. Everybody else in the line would never catch up and would wear out in the long run.

Shop production could be similar in that if you failed to meet earlier set process completion dates, the burden of "catch-up" falls on later processes, like finishing and assembly for example. Those departments can burn out trying to fix scheduling mistakes made by earlier departments while maintaining current production expectations.

Now factor in the intangibles of letting something slip until the last minute or trying to slip, or compress, two-weeks worth of production into one-week. That factor being: when everything has to go perfectly, nothing goes right. Every little miscue is exaggerated by the need for absolute perfection. Sticking to a well thought out plan avoids the pitfalls of compressing everything into the last minute.

If reading and re-reading the initial solicitation was important, reviewing and re-reviewing the bid documents before submittal was super important. Patti was led to understand that while commercial customers were usually understanding and forgiving of discrepancies, the government may not be. It wasn't that the government personnel were ogres, the sheer numbers and complexity of the process didn't allow for even easily preventable errors to be corrected. After all, if the error could have been pre-vented earlier, why hadn't it been prevented before the government processed it with the error, usually in the bidder's favor if it led to the award?

One mistake is bad enough but a few mistakes will definitely not impress the government procurement community. Patti wondered if it was possible to develop a past performance record before even winning a single contract. If it was possible, it couldn't be good.

Patti and Bill made a generic checklist of what should have been done on the rough draft of their quote before submitting:

- Reviewed?

- Standards and specifications satisfied?

- Part numbers verified?

- Packaging requirements satisfied?

- Math double-checked?

- Delivery dates doable?

- All amendments understood, addressed and acknowledged?

- Any contract specific questions answered by the contracting office?

- Any general questions answered by the PTAC? (also, refer to the high-lighted form of "must complete this data" information).

- Contract signed?

- Allowed return time commensurate with method of returning?

- Re-reviewed?

Other types of quotes in the future might dictate other types of final checklists but these questions were adequate for now. The most important factor in Patti's mind was to allow enough time to have the experts at the PTAC a chance to review it.

Patti had been talking to one of the people in particular at the PTAC and felt like they had a good working relationship going. They had never met in person but Patti had always made sure to try and find the answers to her questions before calling her new friend at the PTAC. It made Patti feel like she wasn't wasting anyone's time on obvious questions and it made the PTAC person more receptive to assisting Patti. More than once already, Patti had gotten answers from the PTAC which, if she had called the Contracting Officer, wouldn't have instilled any confidence in the CO towards Techno-Systems.

In fact, no one at Techno-Systems was allowed to contact the contacting office by any method unless they checked with Bill first. If each person of the team contacted the contracting office, in theory there could be six contacts in one day. That was not only a probable major inconvenience to the contracting office, it could prove to be what Kevin called a "deal breaker." Bill believed that a deal breaker equated to business what a "fatal error" was to his computer. Neither one might be as bad as they sounded, but why take a chance?

"How's it looking Patti," asked Bill, "any questions?"

"No, not really. I've cross-checked everything on the checklist. Do you still want to do one final check on my work?"

"Yes I'd like to, but only because it's our first one," replied Bill. "I trust you more than me. It's just important to get off on the right foot."

"Okay. We're on the home stretch then. This last part won't take too long." And it didn't. Patti had everything ready for signing, Bill signed his name, Patti sent it off, and that was that until the government made a decision.

It seemed somewhat anticlimactic after so much thought had gone into reaching this point. Bill decided that Techno-Systems *would* be awarded the contract. Ah, the power of positive thinking. He again quoted one of his favorite profundities: "No sense being pessimistic. It wouldn't work anyway." And who was Patti to say he was wrong?

Bill considered the statistics of the bidders located in his state while he reflected on his chances of being awarded the contract they were working on so hard. Their state was midway on the last *Department of Defense Prime Contract Awards by State* list he had found, where else, on the internet. While it wasn't a deciding factor, Bill did notice an upward trend in the dollar volume over the last few years for the state where Techno-Systems was located.

The top five states were California (15%), Texas, Virginia, Florida and Connecticut. The bottom five states were South Dakota, West Virginia, Montana, Delaware and Wyoming. What it all meant to Bill was the potential for Techno-Systems, or anyone else for that matter, to be a viable supplier to the U.S. Government. He noted that the figures included almost all of the contracts awarded and that the contract work was not necessarily performed in the state where the contract was awarded. That made sense.

Bill thought again of the billions of dollars spent by the government each year and how a drop in the bucket for them could be a tsunami for Techno-Systems. The more that he read about the current situation, the more he sensed the possible more favorable trend for the government to work more with domestic small businesses.

For example, a *Clean Contracting Act* had recently been proposed wherein the bill sought to clean up government procurement in several ways, including:

- Banning monopoly contracts

- Reducing the use of cost-plus contracts

- Prohibiting "layer cake" deals that inflate costs through tiers of subcontractors

- Limiting noncompetitive contracts

- Increasing oversight, and preventing unjustified award fees

- Deterring corruption in contracting

Bill wasn't necessarily sure of what each point meant although they sounded good for small businesses. The Coalition for Government Procurement may have wanted to reverse the trend for the last few years that seemed tilted towards big business. If that was the case, it would be about time.

If reform was coming, Techno-Systems wanted everything in place to take advantage of it if and when it happened. Bill had determined much earlier that all governments, local, state and federal, would be under additional scrutiny as the financial resources got tighter. People, government and taxpayers, preferred to ignore the problem of dwindling money available until it bit them in the butt by running out "all of a sudden." Of course, there was nothing sudden about it to any small business fiscally responsible enough to avoid falling into a situation like that. It simply called for basic business planning.

Bottom line was, if Techno-Systems didn't receive any contracts immediately, they'd just keep trying. Persistence and patience.

If Bill didn't want to try his patience, he wouldn't waste his time or the government's by returning a bid, only to have it arbitrarily rejected for an easily preventable reason. How can a company prevent such rejection? The government had provided tips to avoid just that, the bid:

- Must be kept basic. Resist the urge to get fancy with booklet covers or whatever.

- Must be marked and sealed. All bids are required to be sealed. If it is not sealed, it will not be accepted by the agency.

- Must be identified on the envelope with the bid name and number, or they won't know what it is.

- Must be delivered to the proper place, identified in the bid.

- Must be received by the proper date. Bids received after the closing date will not be considered and will be returned unopened.

- Must be received by the proper time, in the agency's time zone.

- Must be signed. If not, it will be considered non-responsive.

- Must be on the required forms as directed by the agency or be considered non-responsive.

- Must include all other required forms; bid bonds, non-collusion affidavits, deviation sheets, questionnaires, etc. or be considered non-responsive.

- Must acknowledge any and all addenda; amendments, changes, etc. or be considered non-responsive.

- Pricing must be in the required units or be considered non-responsive.

- Any deviations from specification must be identified. At this point, the deviation had better be accepted and acknowledged by the CO as well.

- Quotes submitted by computer must follow the guidelines as required.

If the bid is declared as non-responsive for any of the above issues, it will not be given further consideration, and everybody concerned has wasted time. Bill planned on contacting the PTAC for a final check, at least until he felt more comfortable and confident with Patti's and his judgment.

14

Contract Award

An important point to remember is that being awarded a contract is just the beginning in a few different ways. The first beginning is first impression you give the procurement community of how sincere you are by having done your homework. Try to avoid contacting the Contracting Officer, contracting office or contracting agency with questions you shouldn't have to ask them. It's better to try to find the answer on your own and verify it with your PTAC if you're not sure. While it may not be noticed if you don't bother the buyer too much, it will be if you do. If it's a question only the CO can answer, then, by all means, make contact. The idea is to make your activity as pain-free for the government as possible.

Your performance history is just beginning. Make sure everything is done on time, to regulatory and specification requirements. A bad first performance could also be the last as all activity is documented and will follow you for a long time to come.

And if you do everything right, the best beginning is new relationship you'll be cultivating with Uncle Sam, only the biggest customer in the entire world! A customer that's not seasonal or subject to economic fluctuations. Actually, the tighter the economy, the more possibilities for small businesses because of the additional maintenance, repair and supplementing of current equipment and technology. New equipment and technology most often goes to the super primes or the companies that introduced the new equipment or technology and they will have a corner on the market for awhile. Whatever else may be happening, our government will go on, making it "recession proof."

Two and a half months had passed without a peep from the government. Patti was curious but Bill was too busy to give it much thought until Patti asked him why there was such a rush earlier and so quiet now.

"I don't know, Patti. You probably shouldn't check again though."

"I only called that one time, when they said to be patient. Besides, could it hurt for them to know we're still very interested?"

"The person at the PTAC had a good feeling so let's just hang in there and not bug anyone. If we get it we get it. I'd rather get the second quote anyway, if we only got one or the other."

The second solicitation Techno-Systems had submitted a bid on was a little smaller in dollar volume but even better suited to their operation. There had been a couple of other possibilities to quote on although Techno-Systems was in a position to be fussy about what they'd pursue right then. The second bid was just too perfect to pass on, even though it was for a different agency than the first bid.

Bill wanted to stick with one agency to learn their "ins and outs" but you know that old piano tuner named Upperknockity saying: "Upperknockity tunes only once." He decided to follow the opportunity when it first presented itself. The first bid was to the DoD, the most popular agency it seemed. The second bid was to the Department of Energy (DoE), the department not as big but still purchasing between $18 to $20 billion worth of goods and services annually.

Bill was still the designated prospector at Techno-System because it was relaxing, to him, and maybe comforting, to see all of those opportunities every three days or so. The DoE intrigued him the most lately. Bill had done his usual search on the internet and liked what he found. That was the first thing Bill did when he considered a new government agency or commercial account: visit their website. It didn't take long and Bill learned something worthwhile every time.

Bill had started checking the FBO at home on his old computer and at first it was adequate. As he evolved into more complicated solicitations with multiple websites to visit, he exceeded his old pc's capacity and had to upgrade the system. Apparently, the computer couldn't deal with so many open files. Bill's computer person explained that if you imagined your actual desk as having drawers of information, and each time you opened a drawer you spread the contents on the top of the desk, eventually you could run out of desk top space. Everything in the next drawers would stay in the drawers.

So Bill brought a newer pc from work to his house and between activities with Patti and the girls, Becky and Britney, spent some of his free time in his home office. The sheer number and diversity of the opportunities never failed to amaze him. There had to be something for absolutely every type of supplier wanting to do business with the federal government. Bill had decided that while government contracting wasn't for everybody, there were opportunities for pretty much everybody if they felt so inclined.

Because of the information available on the internet (free), and the agency specific website assistance (free), and the assistance from the PTAC and SBA (free), you couldn't beat the cost of investigating the government marketplace. Compared to going after commercial business, it was, well, almost free. Bill didn't think there was a less expensive market to investigate. Nothing ventured, nothing gained. While it was true that government business wasn't easy, if a company never even explored the possibilities, it was next to impossible to ever do business with the government.

Shortly after pondering those thoughts, Bill found out that Techno-Systems had been awarded their first contract. Beautiful! Here Bill was justifying the efforts put forth so far and the actual first contract announcement validated them. Another good sign, thought Bill.

Patti gave him a big hug and a kiss after she had come in to his office and closed the door. She was even more excited than Bill although, in all fairness, she had been closer to the whole project for the last few months. Bill called a meeting of the other people who had been involved the most, Kevin, Jeremy and Bill Sexton, and told them the milestone news. After advising the team, Bill held an informal company meeting to share the news with the rest of the people. To be successful fulfilling the contract, Bill wanted the entire company to understand the benefits to Techno-Systems.

Bill had scheduled another quick meeting early the next morning to kick off the implementation of the carefully laid plans and to firm up the individual assignments. It was easy because they didn't have to figure out what to do next. If any internal meeting, other than more involved presentations, ever took longer than 15 minutes, Bill would get antsy and question people as to why they weren't better prepared.

This was great, thought Bill. The longest lead-time in Techno-Systems' history, according to Patti, and the profit looked fair, especially for the first order. Being awarded the first contract bid on was against the odds, but if improbable, obviously possible, because here was Techno-System, new supplier to the biggest, toughest, most prestigious customer in the world.

Another month passed with everything still looking good for the first contract's schedule right on time. Patti was already working on her and Bill's favorite part, getting paid. Kevin had been working on taking the ISO Quality System to the next step, ISO Certification. Jeremy's assignment of producing the product hadn't actually started yet although all of the preliminary steps were in place. Bill Sexton was the furthest ahead because all he had to do was to alert the packaging contractor, who had assured him that they would be in with everything two weeks before the scheduled ship date. It was a little earlier than necessary but Bill S. had worked it out with them to ensure compliance before the last minute. Just in case, for Sexton's peace of mind.

The product being produced was an assembly of components to be retrofitted to machines already in use, and was as close to production as Techno-Systems usually saw as a manufacturer. The packaging contractor had submitted drawings of the wooden crates to be utilized over a waterproof wrapping over protective wrapping plus the necessary identification. Way overly simplified in description because, in detail, was ten pages long.

As usual, all of the other day-to-day functions occurring at Techno-Systems continued and Bill was adding more employees to keep up. He recalled worrying about how to keep the original twenty-five employees when he had made a conscious decision to increase Techno-Systems' account base. They now had thirty-eight fulltime employees, including the seven from Systems-Plus, and four part-time. Techno-Systems' growth would be curtailed if they had too much turnover or didn't maximize what they had now.

Employee relations had always been better there than most companies Bill was familiar with, but he knew the bigger they got, the less personal that relationship might be. Jeremy had already given Bill a heads-up on some minor rumblings from second shift. He suggested addressing any issues during the annual employee reviews.

Employee reviews, mused Bill. Until now, they had usually meant a cup of coffee with each employee and a preset across-the-board bump in pay. Bill had been proactive with the members of his management team and had planned a percent or two above the inflation rate increase for all the others.

It hadn't been that long ago when Bill had been in everyone else's safety-toe shoes. He remembered the rate of exchange for the good things they did and the mistakes they made. About ten to a hundred "Atta Boys" could be negated by a single "Aw Shit." It was a cruel world.

Bill had been learning lately that it didn't take any longer to do the job right. He decided that if they were going to go through the process any-way, why not make it more effective for all concerned, the employees and the company. The last time performance reviews came up, Bill had gone to the office supply store and picked up standard "Employee Performance Review" forms with generic criteria to evaluate the employees' attributes and shortcomings. But when Bill looked at the forms, none of the content applied to anyone at the company, except maybe one of the two secretar-ies.

Those forms were still in the file because, not being applicable, they were never used and Bill ended up having a cup of coffee with each employee and then gave them a standard bump. Where had he heard that before? This year was a year of change and Bill had always felt the people who did the work were Techno-Systems' greatest assets. Those valuable assets should grow with the company to keep everything balanced.

Bill's creative juices were flowing to the extent he roughed-out a draft of pertinent evaluation questions, got input from the management team, and gave them to Patti, the company scribe. She formatted the content to short, easy to understand questions like: *Do you clean around your work area at the end of each shift?* or *Are you punctual and on time everyday?* The employee being reviewed would have adequate time to complete the set of twenty or so questions as to how they rated for each question.

The actual performance review would include the employee, the immediate supervisor, and Bill. If the employee's answer didn't agree with the supervisor's or Bill's impressions, it would be a point for discussion and, if necessary, correction. The system could favor the employee if it would bring positive attention to the good things that the employee did which were never acknowledged by management. Vice versa if the employee had negative issues to bring to their attention. Whatever the outcome, issues would be brought out and put on the table for discussion.

Bill had always made a conscious effort to not let any employee become "transparent" because they might be so effective and dependable all the time as to be taken for granted. A really good employee was always just there and their work was always just right. This new review system would remind management what a great employees they were.

Exceptional people were acknowledged, financially when possible, and people who had to change would have the opportunity to set goals for correction. All this good stuff and the review would be so structured throughout most of it that it shouldn't take anymore time than the old way.

Less than a week after Techno-Systems had completed all of the annual employee performance reviews and a little over a month since winning their first contract, Techno-Systems won their second contract.

Bill couldn't help but think that things were going too well. Everything in Bill's life seemed to be exceeding his wildest expectations. All that plus the Dennis Bell case was cleared a few weeks ago. Talk about anticlimactic, although it did cost Techno-Systems an employee. In a perfect world, Donny would have been the guilty party but, even though it would have made Bill feel, for some odd reason, vindicated and saved a good employee, albeit closet killer type, it wasn't to be.

Denny didn't have many friends and few relatives, but one of those relatives was the only one who could love a sneak like Denny, his mother, Ma Bell. She recalled some animosity between her loving son and one of the employees who left Techno-Systems to work at Systems-Plus. Detective Kahler spoke again to the eight employees that had gone to Denny's new company for more money. Donny, the malcontent, was the most likely suspect but it turned out to be Dave Ciszek, coincidentally one of those "transparent" employees.

Dave thought he could be tolerant of Denny's quirks for the extra money, but it was just too much for Dave to contain. Dave always disliked the way Denny's talk went into the gutter whenever he spoke to him, like he had to talk down to anyone in the shop, especially Dave it seemed. Denny would be civil with customers when he brought them through and then would "swear up a blue streak" when it was just him and the manufacturing employee. Dave swore more than Denny so what really offended Dave was being talked down to, like he was a lesser person.

That in itself was nothing, until Dave confronted Denny on a Friday night after everyone else had left. The conversation took a bad turn, things were said and blown out of proportion, Dave pushed Denny out of his face, and Denny slapped Dave and fired him on the spot. That simple and that quick. Dave's pride was terminally damaged and he planned on scaring Denny to teach him a lesson he'd never forget.

Dave requested a meeting to, in Denny's mind anyway, beg for his job back, that coming Sunday at Systems-Plus. To seal the deal, Dave had brought a pint of whiskey, the good stuff, and Denny hadn't noticed that he was the only one actually drinking it. It was heavily drugged and Denny actually sat on the table himself when he became dizzy and disoriented. Dave helped Denny lay back with the encouragement, "it will pass." He positioned an unconscious Denny in the middle of the water jet table and tied his hands and feet sort of spread eagled, but nothing fancy as Denny was dead to the world, or at least on his way. He had planned on just having Denny wake up tied to the bed of the machine but instead, on a whim, pushed the start button, grabbed the hooch, and walked away. Dave was relieved when he found out later that the action of the water jet had somehow washed most traces of the drug away. Perfect.

If Denny had woken up sooner or if Dave didn't have such a dark side that even he didn't know about, the outcome would have been a lot different. Bill was too nice of a guy to ever admit it, but it sure worked out well for him. Patti was better off as well because she could close out that part of her life. A pleasant surprise for Patti was finding out that Denny had forgotten to take her name off his fat life insurance policy and Patricia Bell was still named as the primary beneficiary. Without anyone else, other than Denny's elder mother who wasn't interested, no one contested the payout.

15

Getting Paid

Was there any sweeter aspect to being a small business than getting paid? Not for Patti, and even though Bill had said it was his favorite part, he hardly knew when the checks came in anymore. His accounts receivables, unless a large account was in arrears and Bill wanted to be involved, were completely separate from what he wanted to do on a daily basis. Patti, on the other hand, enjoyed totaling deposits so much that after a particularly satisfying day, she'd like to lean back and have a cigarette later, if she smoked.

Bill and Patti enjoyed going to casinos a couple of times a year if they were nearby anyway. They only played the quarter slots until they each either 1.) lost $20 or 2.) doubled the $20, the former usually being the case. Neither really cared because Patti mostly played for hearing the sound of the payouts tinkling into the tray and Bill just liked to see Patti's face while she savored the tinkling sound. Small pleasures are also sweet.

Along with the informal title of "Company Scribe" for her writing skills, Patti was assigned the task of understanding how the government would pay Techno-Systems. She researched Wide Area Workflow (WAWF), the system adopted by the DoD, since the first transaction would be getting paid on the DoD contract.

This is what she found:

> **Background:** Traditionally, the DoD acquisition process has been paper-based, labor intensive, and heavily dependent upon manual and repetitive data inputs from multiple functional communities. The DoD Paperless Contracting initiative was created in response to the DoD Comptroller's Management Reform Memorandum #2 of 21

May 1997—Moving to a Paper-free Contracting Process. The DoD WAWF began as a Paperless Contracting prototype application to eliminate paper from the Receipt/Acceptance and Invoice/Payment process of the DoD contracting life cycle. It became operational in FY99.

What is DoD WAWF: WAWF is a secure Web-based system for electronic invoicing, receipt and acceptance. WAWF creates a virtual folder to combine the three documents required to pay a Vendor—the Contract, the Invoice, and the Receiving Report. The WAWF application enables electronic form submission of invoices, government inspection, and acceptance documents in order to support DoD's goal of moving to a paperless acquisition process. It provides the technology for government contractors and authorized DoD personnel to generate, capture, and process receipt and payment-related documentation, via interactive Web-based applications. Authorized DoD users are notified of pending actions by e-mail and are presented with a collection of documents required to process the contracting or financial action. It uses Public Key Infrastructure (PKI) to electronically bind the digital signature to provide non-refutable proof that the user (electronically) signed the document with the contents. More importantly, WAWF helps to mitigate interest penalty payments due to lost or misplaced documents and highlights Vendor offered discounts so that the DoD benefits on both fronts, in addition to streamlining the whole process from weeks to days or minutes. Benefits include online access and full spectrum view of document status, minimized re-keying and improving data accuracy, eliminating unmatched disbursements and making all documentation required for payment easily accessible. WAWF is the system that allows DoD to reach its e-invoicing goals and reduce interest penalties due to lost or misplaced documents.

The lights went on in Patti's brain. Aha! The information that she had entered on the Central Contractor Registration (CCR) electronic forms "way back when" became more relevant now. Patti found an unusual comfort in tying some of her efforts together. Bill had brought back information on WAWF installation and registration from the PTAC seminar he had attended. While Patti didn't quite comprehend the instruction sheets, she planned on contacting her contact at the PTAC she was working with for clarification.

So, it seemed to Patti, there was a method to the madness of the whole process. Without all of the paperwork that Bill had threatened Patti with earlier, her job would be easier. In all fairness to Bill though, he did say that the whole process would be different than when he had worked at his old employer years ago. The only downside she could see right now was the payment going directly to the bank instead of across her desk. It was self-serving to like that aspect of the transaction and to miss it although it did save time. Maybe she could read the bank statements for her thrills instead.

Electronic Funds Transfer (EFT) was how the government paid the vendor rather than snail-mailing the check nowadays. Patti related this process back to the banking data she entered into the CCR database earlier. Again, it all made sense. Techno-Systems bank had suggested using direct deposit for their payroll but, so far, Bill was resisting until they got bigger, if even then. Bill enjoyed handing-out the payroll checks personally to keep in contact with each employee. In fact, he tried to make his rounds in the plant (his new term for the shop) at the beginning of each shift. It was his opportunity to "touch" each person, not physically of course, but by saying "Hello" or "Good Morning" or whatever. Nice touch.

The government is required to pay a small business invoice within 30 days of receipt of the invoice. All paperwork or electronic information must be properly submitted by the vendor. Patti planned on visiting the WAWF website for instructions for self-registration even though she had read the PTAC information on the subject and considered it more than adequate. She did decide to take the online course at the WAWF website well before the scheduled ship date though.

Patti had another special project to work on besides getting paid. Bill Sexton was not very computer savvy so he asked if either Patti or Bill Nelson could check on how to buy government surplus direct from the government for resale. It was almost automatic that Patti was the selected as lucky candidate. Bill Sexton's nephew became interested in the subject after his uncle described what huge opportunities *his uncle*, Uncle Sam, had for anyone with a little moxie. Sexton's nephew could have looked it up himself but Bill had been bragging about Techno-System's expertise in the government marketplace and one thing led to another....

So, here was the helpful Patti, stuck with something she wasn't even interested in, until she had gotten into it a little further. Then it actually was a little fun because it was like shopping for really weird items at a really huge flea market. Unbelievable, she thought. Opportunities abound whether you're selling to or buying from the government. She found opportunities from local and state government as well as federal.

One constant thread ran through the surplus marketplace however and the concept wasn't new but extremely important with the government: *Buyer Beware.* Read everything very carefully and make sure you understand what you're bidding on and the terms attached to the sale. FOB points and freight costs can kill more than just your expected profit. Sure, many items were purchased for pennies on the dollar although if a small business bid on a lot of stuff without knowing if they won the bid for awhile, it can add up to a lot of money and obligation if and when they all popped.

Online auctions were probably a better way to start than onsite auctions unless the onsite auction is located close to the buyer. The federal government typically uses their auction website at gsa.gov/auctions while the military uses govliquidation.com although Patti didn't have high hopes of the websites being correct for very long. She'd advise using a search engine for the most current sites, federal, state or local.

There were some stories that, true or just part of the legends surrounding the government marketplace, were interesting nonetheless. Supposedly in Idaho, a car dealer was reselling the major components of a nuclear reprocessing plant to make bomb grade plutonium. High ranking federal officials in Washington, D.C. feared that the resellers' determination to sell nuclear hardware could damage national security. But the car dealer had merely bought the scary stuff from the federal government through a private contractor for $154,000 (the government had paid $10,000,000).

Another story was about a surplus dealer in Miami who bought surplus from Cape Canaveral and found among the purchases a ballast disc for a missile made, in part, from Uranium. The surplus dealer demonstrated to the press the properties of Uranium by scraping his knife on the disc to make showers of sparks. NASA people later paid him a visit and bought back the disc although stating that the Uranium content was "not enough to cause worry."

Another missile related story took place in the late 1970's, when our nuclear arsenal was converted from liquid to solid fuel. Patti remembered hearing about when the U.S. Government auctioned off a number of missile silos and their contents, mostly the silos were then used for grain storage. One of the missiles was offered at a sealed bid auction and purchased by an undergraduate student at MIT for $3,000.

He requested that the government deliver, at their expense, the missile to the nearest military base to him. He then arranged for a truck from there and donated the missile to a local modern art museum. Tax laws at the time allowed him to deduct the original value of the missile (major bucks) instead of the price he paid ($3,000). Income averaging allowed him to spread the "loss" out over a number of years so he didn't have to pay taxes for a long time.

Very interesting, thought Patti, and just last night she had read about military surplus in the evening newspaper. The DoD had donated nearly 380,000 pieces of unneeded military equipment, from trucks, boats and M-14 rifles to combat boots, to 16,000 cash strapped local police agencies. Included were fully automatic M-16 rifles, large stationary power generators, helmets, 12-passenger vans, a $55,000 24' boat (it cost only $50 to repair and $500 for shipping), and other "assorted oddball things."

Didn't Bill just tell me the Army, Marines and National Guards were running out of stuff? Patti wondered why the DoD would be giving stuff away if they'd just probably have to re-buy it later but such things were beyond what she cared about.

It was a huge market with every imaginable item for sale or open for bidding on. Federal and military surplus, outdated or excess, and items seized by the government for any number of reasons. Patti noted vacant land, houses, cars, trucks, motorcycles, boats, engines, office supplies, electronics, cameras, tools, etc., etc. There was way too much to list so Patti made a few page copies and passed them on to Bill Sexton.

"Thanks, Patti,"

"You're welcome, Mr. Sexton." Patti liked Bill Sexton, but didn't everybody? Sure, he was the butt of a lot jokes although it was never mean-spirited and the jokesters were always well-intentioned. Bill always laughed *with* everyone.

"Hey, what do you think of this idea? Oops, I appreciate the good work on the surplus, but I had another idea for Willy, besides. Willy, he's my nephew. How bout starting a business to help people like Techno-Systems with government business? Besides buying government surplus, foreclosures, tax seized stuff, or whatever."

"It could work, I suppose, but Mr. Nelson would know more about that than me. At first blush, there are lots of opportunities for anyone with an imagination."

"Well that's Willy. He actually had the ideas about both the surplus and the other thing. And he's already got everything he needs, he thinks."

"Actually, all your nephew would need is a fairly decent computer, a *lot* of time to learn what he's doing and the moxie to go out and get some clients, especially if the initial clients weren't too technical, like we are. But the government buys, leases or rents everything imaginable from every type of business. Yes, I think it's doable. In fact, I like it."

"William, my godson nephew, who was even named after me, has already spoken to the SBA lady who was here to see the other Bill. She said William being a veteran, a minority *and* in a HUBZone was advantageous *if* he owned a business, but he just got out of the Marines four months back so that's not going to happen for awhile. She did say that the primes and the government were really looking for Service Disabled Veteran businesses right now, but I'm glad he's just healthy."

"Amen to that," said Patti.

"William has a great imagination and he's always had a lot of drive. Within reason, he already has some financial backing, including me, if he needs it. He thought for now he'd pick up a few clients at one to two-hundred bucks a month each and do web searches for them or whatever. Maybe he'll make an arrangement with one of those clients or see another opportunity as he goes along. Either way, he'll be making some money while he's setting something up."

"I pretty sure the government prefers working with established companies but, nothing ventured, nothing gained. If he's smart and he works hard, well, I've been able to control my life by using my wits, even through the rough times." Patti added, "Maybe Mr. Nelson could even utilize his services someday, after he learned the business of course. I've got a friend at the PTAC. Maybe he should talk to them. They have their finger on the pulse of government needs like the SBA. You said that he's already talked to them?"

"Yeah, and he had a good feeling over the meeting. Said they're good people."

"So are the people at the PTAC. He should start out by attending some of their seminars. He'll not only learn a lot, he'll make some good contacts. Maybe even some future clients."

"William's learning about GSA contracts for an office supply place in town already and he said it hasn't cost him a cent so far. He's still interested in the surplus business but the more he finds out, the more opportunities he sees. Like a kid in a candy store I suppose. He knows it's not as easy as it seems but, like you said, the man's got the moxie to make something work. He'll probably focus on whatever he feels the most comfortable with, for starters."

"Mr. Nelson said, 'The government is farming out more of what they used to do themselves' so I'm sure your nephew will find his niche."

"He will. Hey! Thanks, Patti. You're the greatest."

16

More Contracts

Bill asked everyone on the Management Team to review their personal exposure to the federal government marketplace and requirements, and what their impressions were to date. They were also asked to jot them down for the next weekly meeting. Nothing too elaborate though because of his self-imposed 15 minute maximum length meeting. That always kept everything efficient and effective.

Everyone had done everything necessary to process Techno-Systems first contract to the point they were at now, two weeks from shipping. So far, everything had pretty much gone exactly to plan except for some missing raw material certifications from one of their vendors, but that had been corrected last week. Bill was happy and wanted to give the other members of the team an opportunity for their input. They had all risen to the occasion and could genuinely claim ownership of their participation.

Bill wanted to foster that feeling of ownership by encouraging their ideas. At the next meeting, Bill spoke first:

Bill: "First order of business is, Thank You. We planned what we were going to do, and we did it. The contract for the DoD is coming in a little under budget and I'm happy with that. Everything is right on schedule for shipping complete, it's to spec and the Contract Officer said it went quite well, especially for a first contract. The DoE contract is going okay too except for my mistake on the circuit boards, but we should still almost breakeven. Next time I'll double-check but maybe next time Jim won't be on vacation when I cost it out. We're looking at another DoE bid. What do you folks think? Patti?"

Patti: "Thanks Bill. Completing the contract forms for submittal went well on all five of the quotes we've sent back. Of course you know we were awarded two of those quotes and the last one, lucky number five I hope, is still looking good. On numbers' three and four, as you know, Bill pushed a little more on the profit part to see if we were leaving too much on the table. Number five was quoted the same as three and four but not everyone can do the last one. The DoE is very nice to work with. They're very considerate. That's about all I had. Oh, and I hope we get lucky number five!"

Bill: "Thanks Patti. For every one else's general information., we normally don't talk about profitability but just this once, quotes' three, four and five, had a higher risk value."

Patti: "Oops. Sorry Bill."

Bill: Not a problem. I planned on saying something about it, but, I kept forgetting. Kevin. What do you think?

Kevin: "I've settled on a third party ISO registrar, the best I think, of the three we spoke to, certainly the most responsive. They'll be here in exactly … seven weeks. It could have been sooner if we, or I, had called sooner. We're ready but we're waiting because of their schedule. Two of our biggest commercial accounts are looking forward to our future ISO 9001:2000 registration. I guess they'll feel more comfortable with the tougher jobs. I didn't mind the government's quality assurance requirements. It's been okay so far but ask me again closer to the ship date to the DoD. That's it for me."

Jeremy: "As far as I'm concerned, other than a few old prints from four administrations ago, and a bunch of smaller, busier prints than we're used to, manufacturing wasn't a lot different than our other accounts. If anything was unclear, I'd just give the print to Kevin and ask him how he'd inspect it. I say, if we make enough money for newer equipment with government business, let's do it."

Bill Sexton: "Well, the packaging contractor sent the supplies we needed for the DoD shipment and will bring all of the ID stuff, labels, bar coding and RFID, on the day before our ship date, guaranteed. They honored their quote even though they forgot a desiccant requirement in the original quote to us. I explained we quoted exactly the same price to the government on the first contract. I didn't say anything to them but on future quotes, Bill said we'd bump it up a little to give us a little slack. Because of our bigger product, we'll probably utilize these same guys indefinitely. The DoE shipments don't seem quite as tough as the DoD. I don't mind the government with the help from the pros."

Bill: "Thank you all again. If I hear correctly, there aren't any major problems or reasons to *not* continue this government direction at this time. Right?"

Group: A few head shakes, a murmured "no" and an "uh uh."

Bill: "Any other business?"

Patti: "Oh! I just remembered something that doesn't apply to us but it was in the paper recently. Companies who hire illegal immigrants, even if inadvertently, would be banned from participating in federal contracts for 7-10 years. It wouldn't be subject to appeal in court but the government could waive it for national security reasons. For what it's worth, I guess," shrugging her shoulders.

Bill: "Thanks, Patti, something to keep in mind. Anything else?"

They discussed a few other issues for another 5 minutes and adjourned.

The DoE was not only more receptive to Techno-Systems, they appeared to be genuinely interested in cultivating a relationship. Bill had the opportunity to meet with the Contract Officer for the contract with the DoE. He was encouraged to attend a conference sponsored by them and was registered with the DoE's Industry Interactive Procurement System (IIPS) and the OSDBU Small Business Database. All of these suggestions came directly from the DoE and Bill actually felt as though they wanted to work with him on future projects.

There were still tons of opportunities with all of the other agencies in the federal government, and Bill would continue to check them out although his efforts would be concentrated with the DoE. He suspected that if you could spend time investigating any of the different agencies in depth, you'd find more opportunities than at first blush. The DoE, for example, had many opportunities including purchasing supplies, facility management, remediation, construction, research and development, management and scientific consulting, administrative services, data processing, security, engineering, and waste treatment and disposal, which was close to Techno-Systems' future contracts : waste storage.

Even though Bill had settled on the DoE and the DoD for now and filtered the FBO accordingly, every so often he'd still check the broader system. It was easy to do but something he'd usually only do at home when he had free time because if nothing else, Bill found it mildly entertaining. The various requests were for furniture, remodeling, windows, leased cars, machine tools, metals, home oxygen, rental property, food items, clothing, printing, medical services, seminars, building materials, motorcycles, communication equipment and services, etc., etc. Pretty much everything used in the commercial marketplace was also used in the government marketplace.

If anyone can't find a product or service to provide to the federal government, they're not looking hard enough Bill had been thinking lately. While he wished he had explored all of these opportunities earlier, he was glad to at least be in the marketplace now. Any business owner took risks by the very nature of assuming a businesses' liabilities although Bill couldn't see the downside of investigating the government as a potential customer.

The checking of the FBO periodically confirmed, for Bill anyway, that he was on the right track with the DoE and the DoD. No doubt about it, he would stick with his plan for now so he wouldn't lose focus on where Techno-Systems' best chances of success were. After all, federal contracting was only planned for maybe twenty-five percent of Techno-Systems' total business and the commercial orders had been coming in consistently for a while lately. *If* the government percentage increased, it would not be at the expense of the usually more profitable commercial business.

Although if future situations merited it someday, Bill would adjust for the times. An example for Bill might be an item wherein Techno-Systems would have a distinct advantage over his competitors because of something they developed. If so, then Techno-Systems deserved more profit and would price it accordingly. It would only be fair for all concerned.

Bill was curious of all of the marketing opportunities offered by the government a few months ago. So one night at home he got on the information highway, the internet, and looked up a report on which agencies bought what over a year's time. It was too much to print out but he found website offering millions of pages of data for public use. Everything from agencies' forecasts for future planning to histories of which vendors supplied the government by dollar amounts. When Bill came across a NASA website, it prompted a memory he hadn't thought about for years.

Right after completing his first machining semester, Bill had gone to a machine shop way out in the countryside to apply for work while attending the rest of school. The machine shop's address was listed as rural and Bill found himself at a traditional farm a little further outside of town than he had envisioned. Wondering if he had the wrong place, he double checked the mailbox and sure enough, it had the machine shop's name, but where was the shop?

Then he noticed a well-traveled road leading through a wooded area and drove down to a large modern pole barn with over a dozen vehicles parked beside it. He parked and went in the office to a sight he'd never forget. Pictures of rockets and other space exploration projects from NASA were framed and hung all over the walls of the professionally decorated office. Unbelievable!

Come to find out, this small business in the middle of the woods did work almost exclusively for NASA, other than a few maintenance jobs for some of the local farms in the area. The contrast between the classic farm setting and the highly sophisticated product the company produced was particularly dramatic to young Bill. They had state of the art manufacturing equipment and inspection equipment to make them, in Bill's eyes, a world class operation. Even though Bill didn't accept the machinist's assistant position because it was too far to drive and they preferred a fulltime person, Bill never looked down his nose at any manufacturing facility again.

It now surprised Bill that he had been so close to government contracting in the past without really giving it much thought. In fact, he had worked on a job just a few years ago that hadn't meant much then although it might now. Six years ago, Denny had gotten a job from another local company and Bill had done most of the work on it. The job was ultimately for the U.S. Postal Service although the other local company was a subcontractor and Techno-Systems had been contacted by them to help get the job finished on time for the prime contractor. The prime had been late in getting their bids in from the subs.

The subcontractor's part of a large order was for a subassembly that was part of a larger assembly for the Postal Service and must have been a big contract overall. Bill thought all of the lesser considered agencies, like the U.S. Postal Service, must have things that wear out or the technology updated. He made a mental note to sort of keep an eye out for future requests of the assembly or maybe even investigate the old order for any part numbers. If, by any stroke of luck, it came up again, he'd look into its history. Maybe farm part of it out to the other local manufacturer. That would be ironic, he thought, because they have experience with the assembly but not with working directly with the government.

The scenario made Bill feel somewhat empowered, that he knew the "secrets" to federal contracting and was now a prime contractor in his own right. It also felt like Techno-Systems was a cut above the other local manufacturer even though they had been around forever, had an awesome reputation and was a few times larger. They were also the company that Kevin had borrowed the ISO 9001:2000 Standards from and had been ISO certified for years. And once Techno-Systems had a favorable past performance record, all of the different agencies would be more available to them.

With that in mind, Bill jotted a note to check out the U.S. Postal Service for the assembly rather than trusting his mental note.

Every agency had to buy, lease or rent whatever was necessary to keep them going. Whatever necessary was every imaginable product or service anyone could ever provide. Bill had been considering making government contracting a larger percentage of Techno-Systems than initially planned. While he didn't plan on cutting back his commercial business, if government business rose to be half of Techno-Systems' total sales, Bill wouldn't complain. To the contrary, commercial business was expected to grow as well.

Growing Techno-Systems was not an obsession with Bill but he did *expect* the company to grow in future years. Ah, the power of positive expectations. Techno-Systems had a good start in establishing the necessary criteria to be a world-class organization. For starters, an internationally high standard Quality Program, a sincere and positive management team, and an increasingly stable base from which to grow.

Interesting situation, because Techno-Systems was stable enough at the size they were, they were in a position to grow. It was like the classic situation of not being able to get a loan unless you didn't need it. All of this fit with what Bill was told early on in their pursuit of government business: that if a company needed a government contract to stay in business, the contract will probably pull them under the rest of the way.

Bill looked back on his decision to secure a better commercial customer base before the concerted effort on government business. What could have been a bad experience turned out to be a life-changing event for both Bill and his company. In his case, all of the factors just sort of fell into place, or did they? Bill didn't believe in luck so it wasn't that. What some people called "luck," Bill considered "just the way things happen" although he did observe that "luck" seemed to happen to more people who had a plan.

Bill had a plan and he expected positive results from his plans. His plans now included more government exposure for Techno-Systems and if it produced additional profitable business, it was a go. If all Techno-Systems saw was marginally profitable business for the next couple of years, they didn't need it. Bill expected to make a fair profit on their government contracts or why take that production time away from the commercial market?

So, future contracts were expected but only on Techno-Systems' terms, or more to the truth, Bill's terms at this point in time. Maybe Techno-Systems would grow so big that Bill could sit back and let other, competent people make those decisions, but not now. If he even had the opportunity, would Bill let Techno-Systems grow beyond his ability to maintain his personal knowledge, control and the standards he had set for the company? Or should he push more now and spend more time with the girls later? Patti had joined Becky and Britney in the "girl" status by now. Of course there was a big difference in the girls in that Becky and Britney really needed his attention right now, at ages twelve and fifteen.

Bill made these conscious decisions:

1. To spend more time with Becky and Britney now by doing less hand's-on and legwork for the next five years and delegating more, with appropriate compensation, to his management team.

2. To spend more time with Patti away from the office, maybe some trips with the other girls in his life.

3. To hire a Sales Manager to put together a Sales Department. Hopefully they could find a contracting specialist or invest in training someone for it.

4. To spend more of the time that he did work on working through others and to avoid the day-to-day minutia that tended to drag him down. Big decisions never bothered Bill, the petty crap was a killer though.

5. Set a company-wide goal to be such a great manufacturer that customers would come to them, the people at Techno-Systems.

Future contracts might come to Techno-Systems as well because Bill planned on increasing his personal presence in one area: Marketing. It was something he had always wanted to do but never had time, and now he was going to make time. The marketing plan had been to ship an order to a commercial customer and have it so exceptional that the customer came back for the next order. Still a plan that worked although, to Bill, there was a distinction between sales and marketing. Bill would be more of a Marketing Person, capitalized in his mind.

And to whom would Bill market Techno-Systems? Bill envisioned taking Patti to vendor conferences in Washington D.C. and possibly DoE field sites to either enhance or follow-up on either new contracts or completed contracts. He honestly didn't know how much call there was for what he wanted to do but that was beside the point. The point was that Bill had a plan.

17

All's Well

"The future is now," said Bill at Techno-Systems' Twenty-Fifth Anniversary Celebration Dinner. "We owe all of our successes to you, the whole Techno-Systems' team. Techno-Systems' greatest asset has always been, and will continue to be, the people. In the last twelve-plus years that I've been the owner, we've grown from twenty-five employees to a hundred and sixteen and we're far from finished growing. Four and a half times the employees, and almost twenty times the volume. Outstanding work everyone. Thank you."

No doubt about it, life was good for Bill. Patti and Bill were an old married couple by now and even though she didn't have birth children, Becky and Britney were close to her. Becky had a one-year old little boy so Bill and Patti were grandparents! Little Sam *was her* grandson as far as Patti was concerned and Bill was spending more time with the little guy than he had with his daughters.

Backing off as the only person who could make a decision at Techno-Systems and letting the others in the organization rise to the occasion might have been the key. It was true what Bill had always said about staying out of the way of good employees and letting them do their thing. The only problem was, Bill didn't practice what he preached when he was in the position to be the one getting in the way. He was practicing it now though. He tried to hire the best, compensate them accordingly, and most important, *stay the hell out of their way.*

This philosophy had served him well over the last twelve years. Techno-Systems wasn't the only thing far from done because Bill had ideas to expand his horizons. If the company was ever able to go public, Bill would be very pleased. That had not been the case only ten years ago because Bill wouldn't have relinquished control back then.

Bill had come all this ways and he was still relatively young, fifty-four years old, well, for another month anyway. If anyone would ask Bill what the secret of his success was, he wouldn't know. There is no clear path to financial success for anyone unless you're born rich, which adversely seems to many to be a path to failure at life too. Sometimes to Bill, it seems as though people with a lot of money are happy in spite of being rich, not because of it. Part of Bill's dream was to be a successful businessman, of which being fairly wealthy now could be a yardstick as to how successful he was, not how happy he was.

No, if Bill was happy it wasn't because of his wealth, it was the way he had gotten wealthy. As a matter of fact, Bill *was* happier than he could ever remember because he had taken charge of his life and made some good decisions, both private and business. The choice to pursue government business was a factor in the direction Techno-Systems had gone. He would have done okay without it, but with it the company was either forced into making improvements or made them by enhancing their position in the marketplace.

The net result was that Techno-Systems doing business with the United States Federal Government was good for a lot of people. It had facilitated the change that grew Techno-System to what they were today, a world-class manufacturer and a leader in their industry.

Techno-Systems had received five patents for technology developed from what they were doing for the DoE, or rather *with* the DoE. Both Techno-Systems and the DoE considered their work together as a partner-ship.

Another positive system implemented was inspired by the introspective evaluation that Techno-Systems made on their costing direct labor and machine time to quote and report on government contracts. The old method, seeped in tradition but horribly outdated, was to use the same cost figure for machine time only, without regard to how sophisticated or expensive the machine was or who was operating it. The new system was as easy as ABC, Activity Based Costing.

Activity Based Costing utilized more accurate figures based on the actual cost of a particular machine and the employee group's actual wages plus a benefit's package plus an operating percentage added to the machine and employee figures. For example, the new system reflected the impact that a lower cost helper usually made on an expensive machine's overall cost because it kept the downtime down and the running time up. It also allowed Techno-Systems to evaluate which machines and personnel offered the most bang for the buck on a particular job.

Yes, it seemed most everyone was happy except for poor Dave Ciszek, because he was languishing away in prison, serving a "life" sentence. Patti would have loved this tat, thought Dave, admiring a new prison tattoo of a wolf. Patti might even have a chance to see it sometime as Dave was up for parole in eight more years, maybe less. He had no way of knowing that Patti would be happier if he was dead or that the crude tattoo looked more like a demented Pomeranian on drugs. It was right over the sentiment : "Life is a bitch, and then you die." It summed it all up in Dave's opinion, though two other prisoners sported tats with: "Life is a shit sandwich, and everyday's another bite," and the equally profound: "Life is like a shit sandwich, the more bread you have, the less shit you have to eat."

Definitely less happiness here although Dave was proud of never implicating or even hinting that he and Patti had known each other, a lifetime ago. It had started way back in high school, right there in the same city as Techno-Systems was and where Patti was still living the good life. Dave was a football jock and was a "big man on campus," or in the government parlance Bill Nelson was, according to Patti, always so damn smug about using, a "BMOC." Patti however was a year younger in high school with a mousy, quiet personality. While Dave was Patti's dream boy, he didn't even know she existed.

The infatuation/indifferent situation had reversed itself when, coincidentally, they were brought back together again years later at Techno-Systems when Dave applied for a skilled labor position. Dave was a thirty-seven year old ex-jock loser who still wore his "glory days," his now snug high school letter jacket every day of his life, even if it was hot weather.

Patti was married to the boss, an asshole named Denny Bell. The worm's turned thought Dave. Now he wouldn't have been recognizable except for the tired hero jacket and Patti was the hot item.

They had acknowledged each other and that would have been that except, to Dave's delight, first love dies hard or maybe she felt sorry for him but Patti would visit with him occasionally in the shop. They would visit when Patti was sure no one would overhear them and to his chagrin, asked him to please, please not tell anyone they knew each other. It was probably more accurate to say that Dave might have known *of* her but, way back when, she had dreamed of him often. Funny how things work out, they had both thought at the time although neither voiced it. He never disclosed their secret but thought, "in your face, asshole!" every time Denny might chew him out for something.

More than once Patti had gotten misty when she described her loneliness over Denny chasing other women all the time, and "why isn't this enough?" she'd say while opening her arms as if to draw attention to her total package. Dave was inspired to become a good machinist and had, and when Denny offered him quite a bit more money to come to his new company, Systems-Plus, he jumped. Sure, Denny was an asshole but he was also the asshole who signed his bigger paychecks and after the extra money Dave was making, he didn't seem to wear his letter jacket as often. Didn't need it.

By then, Patti and Denny had gotten a divorce and she had cooled towards Dave. Bitch! Then Patti called him after she had sold Techno-Systems to Bill Nelson and asked to visit him for "old time's sake." She and Dave were closer than ever. Though all was not good in Patti's world, she explained, and Denny had screwed her again. He had left her in debt but at least she was still the primary beneficiary on Denny's life insurance policy, not that it made any difference; Denny was as healthy as a horse. There was nothing Patti could do except move to another city and start over.

Everything else just happened and here was Dave in prison and Patti had, he learned later, married that other sucker, Bill Nelson. Their success seemed to underscore his dismal, miserable life. In eight years, however,

Dave would be eligible for parole and he had been an exemplary prisoner all those years with just that goal in mind, getting out. Thank you overcrowded penal institutions! Thank you dwindling operating money! To his way of thinking, they owed him, especially Patti. Owed him big time.

18

And You?

Is government contracting right for you?
What are the real risks?
Any reason that you wouldn't at least check it out?

Government contracting is possible for almost every company and probable for most. If you're interested, at some point in time there will be opportunities for whatever your expertise and organization. Because the government buys, rents or leases absolutely anything and everything imaginable, the question isn't as much if they use it as when they'll use it. Granted, it could be umpteen years before your opportunity arises and it's not practical to wait for it.

Virtually every action taken has some degree of risk although with the government, the risk is primarily time spent rather than money spent to investigate the marketplace. The risk, as we conventionally think of the term, is if and when a company decides to offer a formal bid. Time *is* money and it could involve a great deal of time, although relatively minimal cash outlay is required if you investigate the government marketplace yourself. If you tried it and found you didn't care for it, simply stop doing it.

If there's so much to gain and so little to lose by just checking it out, why not? The large potential return on minimal investment should merit at least a peek. You can take that peek from any pc at home or from work and training is available for free over the internet or at little or no cost from your PTAC.

And if you're still not interested after reading this book, wait until the timing is right and *then* check it out. It may behoove you investigate the government marketplace sooner than later though because conditions for small businesses might be improving even more soon and you may want to be ready to strike when it's hot.

Between 2000 and 2005, procurement spending became the hottest, fastest growing area of federal discretionary spending. A comprehensive report shows that nearly 40 cents of every dollar spent is on contracts with private companies. A rise of 86 percent and a record level.

It was also reported that noncompetitive contracts rose by 115 percent in the same period. The five largest federal contractors received over 20 percent of the contract dollars awarded and federal spending with Halliburton contracts increased over 600 percent between 2000 and 2005. Unacceptable numbers for small businesses. Unacceptable for every taxpayer as well.

The general public is probably not anti big business but they may be more pro small business after some of the recent bad press on some of the big, familiar primes. If the seemingly out of control spending, or perhaps more accurately, lack of accountability and/or responsibility in government spending, is on the public's mind, the politicians can't be far behind. The politicians are the force to reform the current system.

These are the kind of procurement issues they'll be monitoring closer:

A recent report from the U.S. House of Representatives entitled: *Waste, Abuse, and Mismanagement in Department of Homeland Security Contracts* stated that "With spending rocketing from $3.5b to $10b between 2003 and 2005, and the volume of contracts rising from 14,000 to 63,000 in the same period, the DHS didn't exactly cover itself in glory." Citing:

- 32 *huge* contracts involving significant overcharges, wasteful spending or mismanagement.

- A $10b contract for the US-VISIT border security system was found to rely on out-of-date and ineffective technologies and, even if it worked, might not prove to be very effective.

- Several billion dollars were spent on airport screening and radiation-detection systems that did not work.

How and why did this happen? It depends on who you ask, but the explanations and excuses included:

- *Too much sole-sourcing.* By 2005, more than half (55% or $5.5b) of DHS contracts were awarded without full and open competition. By contrast, back in 2003, more than 4 out of 5 DHS followed an open, competitive procurement process. Put another way, uncompetitive contracts grew by over 700% in 3 years.

- *Vague requirements.* Too often, the DHS would issue RFPs with vague, fluffy, poorly defined requirements. In one example, bidders were told that "We're asking you to come back and tell us how to do our business ..."

- *Too little training.* The department simply didn't have enough trained procurement staff to keep up with the rapidly growing spend.

Not a pretty picture. The committee chairman called it: "acquisition dysfunction," but the bottom line is that the winds of change are coming and you could be part of the solution.

Another troubling report indicates the worsening situation of the Congress recommended, SBA monitored percentage of federal business to be awarded to small businesses. The "at least" 23% was actually 20% in 2004 and 17% in 2005 according to Eagle Eye Publishers, a Fairfax, VA based firm that helps vendors build relationships with government buyers. The DoD is thought to be the main factor in driving down the small businesses share. Large firms purchasing small businesses with current federal contracts also impacts the 23% goal.

A new rule in the works would require all small businesses receiving contracts through preference awards to report any mergers or acquisitions that will affect the initial size of their business within 30 days. A new regulation would also require long-term contract holders to report any updates in the size of their businesses every 5 years.

The American Small Business League President, Lloyd Chapman, has stated: "White House PR firms have been working overtime to kill stories on Bush administration policies that have diverted over $300 billion in federal small business contracts to the top 2 percent of U.S. firms." A 2006 Office of Government Accountability report found the current administration had spent $1.6 billion over 30 months on public relations campaigns and advertising. That's over $50 million a month to some of the nation's largest public relations firms!

The current administration had also been notoriously secretive, manipulative and vindictive to anyone seeking answers to the suspect procurement practices. In fact, it would seem that the federal government expected all to bend their knee and not ask for any accountability however as journalists sloughed off accusations of picking on the administration, other methods might have been devised.

Although we live in the information age, is it possible that "hush money" could hamper efforts to expose billions if fraud and abuse in federal small business contracting programs? If so, taxpayer's money is being spent to both help and hinder the process to involve small businesses to the SBA's stated goals.

Yet another questionable practice regards the probable sacrifices tolerated by the government to make sure certain primes are accommodated. Recently, the U.S. Army decided to wait 3-4 years for an established U.S. prime to develop technology that is already available now from an Israeli manufacturer. The question is, are good soldiers dying because of a relationship between the government and a prime? If so, there's another area where fresh technology may be discouraged while an established prime, an "old friend of the Army," is given an unfair opportunity. Certainly not fair for the soldiers.

Good old boy networks have actually increased in strength over the last few years because there are cases where the extra money has been made available without enough qualified personnel to spend it or enough qualified projects to spend it on. An example of this is the money wasted in the Katrina debacle and the money "lost" in other countries during actions implemented.

While the majority of federal employees are undoubtedly conscientious, the minority, the bad ones, cause the bad press that reflects poorly on the whole system. Examples are the following results of a House Armed Services Committee finding:

- The Pentagon paid $20 each for $.99 plastic ice cube trays to buy from a DLA approved vendor.

- The Pentagon paid $1,000 each for hot plates when previously the same ones were purchased at $450. The difference? No competition.

- Generally standard 34-inch refrigerators were purchased in the spring of 2004 by the Pentagon for $22,797 each.

The House Armed Services Committee called the buyers for the Pentagon incompetent, initiating an internal review by the DoD of the prime vendor system. The result? The DLA agreed to seek out more competitive bids, but only among the pre-selected vendors on their preferred list. Not a root cause solution.

There are plenty of different blogs on government business practices but you can't be sure of how much to actually believe. It's hard to pick out the sour grapes from legitimate complaints so rumors and bad attitudes could have accounted for some of the unflattering reports. You've probably read things about big primes like: "Over two hundred years of tradition unhampered by progress" and, "you can buy better but you can't pay more." Even President Bill Clinton once commented on "supporting yesterday's technology tomorrow." Although whether everything good or bad you read is totally true isn't the big issue, the fact is people probably *believe* it is. Perception is truth.

If politicians start actually listening to those people who are unhappy with the current system, again, change may be in the wind; change in favor of small business. This is not exactly a new thought because, years ago, the then outgoing President of the United States, President Dwight D. Eisenhower presented a speech. While the president didn't use the term "prime contractor," the language could have applied to them as part of the military/industrial relationship he had been cautioning against. The speech was entitled: *Military-Industrial Complex Speech, Dwight D. Eisenhower, 1961.* This excerpt is interesting:

> "Until the latest of our world conflicts, the United States had no armaments industry. American makers of plowshares could, with time and as required, make swords as well. But now we can no longer risk emergency improvisation of national defense; we have been compelled to create a permanent armaments industry of vast proportions. Added to this, three and a half million men and women are directly engaged in the defense establishment. We annually spend on military security more than the net income of all United States corporations."

> "This conjunction of an immense military establishment and a large arms industry is new in the American experience. The total influence—economic, political, and even spiritual—is felt in every city, every State house, and every office of the Federal government. We recognize the imperative need for this development. Yet we must not fail to comprehend its grave implications. Our toil, resources and livelihood are all involved; so is the very structure of our society."

> "In the councils of government, we must guard against the acquisition of unwarranted influence, whether sought or unsought, by the military-industrial complex. The potential for the disastrous rise of misplaced power exists and will persist."

These insightful observations of the military/industrial relationship so long ago have not only become true, it's almost traditional by now. Some of the largest prime contractors supply the newest American technology to the government on an ongoing basis simply because it is expected. They are aggressively supported by the politicians from their states and districts. Military bases around the country were closed to save money although it seemed as if the states not supporting the current administration were hit the hardest. The administration influenced the military, and the military influenced the primes which were awarded the most business. Free enterprise with the real backbone of this country, small businesses, was also influenced, for the worse.

The net result *is* the annual U.S. Military budget is almost as much as the rest of the world combined. The most current figure was $441.6 billion annually plus $41.1 billion annually for Homeland Security funding *plus* $100 billion for the wars in Iraq and Afghanistan. The last figure, $100 billion, was not even officially part of the regular budget, probably just absorbed into the operating cost.

We, as citizens of the greatest country on earth, do not take such huge figures seriously because we've become accustomed to them. We're comfortable with accepting billion dollar amounts spent by our government, in part, because it's always been that way, almost traditional. Remember how much a billion really is:

- One billion seconds ago, it was 1975.

- One billion minutes ago, Jesus Christ walked the earth.

- One billion pennies stacked on each other would be almost 1,000 miles high.

- One billion dollars laid end-to-end would encircle the earth almost four times.

- One billion dollars to the U.S. Government is less than eight hours spending.

Billions are spent on the future technology we *might* need someday but there are even bigger needs right now. Today's technology in the field needs maintenance *now* to keep our soldiers safer and effective. It was recently stated that the Army, Marines and National Guard are running dangerously low on everyday supplies and the repair parts necessary to keep their military machine(s) working. Small businesses have historically been providing many of those supplies and repair parts although re-supply has, at times, been put back in favor of future super technology. The real "canaries in the coal mine" are the recent changes in the Congress and Senate; a cry from the American public for budget shifts.

In all fairness, new technology has been facilitated by more and more small businesses than in the past and is perhaps one of the government's largest growth areas. Is the timing right for small businesses supplying either maintenance or new technology in either products or services? If you get into the mix earlier, you'll be better able to position yourself to take advantage of future opportunities. While it may not be the best opportunity in America since the discovery of gold at Sutter's Mill, there's easily more potential for those willing to invest a little time in mining.

The United States is now the largest debtor in the world, a major fall from being the largest creditor, and if future government budgets are cut or spending deferred until the deficit gets caught up, small businesses may benefit more than big businesses. The overall indications are that the government climate will most likely favor smaller businesses in the more immediate future. Big prime contractors are, and will continue to be, necessary to keep the United States the most powerful country in the world, although current public sentiment seems to favor spreading the opportunities around.

The final points are these: If you don't at least consider the possibilities of government contracting for your small business, you'll never know. The best time to investigate is sooner than later. The U.S. Government will be buying something from someone and it could just as well be you.
Author's Note:

Thank you for buying this book and for obviously finishing it.

The "how to" aspect of the book hopefully inspires you to give serious consideration to what our favorite uncle, Uncle Sam, can do for you and your business.

Please remember, you don't need luck, you need patience and persistence to succeed. What some people call luck may be better described by a quote from Louis Pasteur in 1854: *"Where observation is concerned, chance favours only the prepared mind."* Make your own "luck" and succeed.

Visit my website at www.fccllc.com or write:

Federal Contract Consultants, LLC
619 No. Moonlight Dr.
Altoona. WI 54720-1420

The fiction aspect of the book didn't seem quite complete so I added an epilogue of how the main characters will be doing in the future. The year is 2025 ...

19

Epilogue: Year 2025

Dave Ciscek took a step outside the Midvale Prison for the first time in almost 19 years. The day wasn't like he'd been picturing in his mind: dark, foggy, maybe raining, basically shitty weather. He'd walk slowly through the drizzle, not caring if he got soaked. Walking with his head held high, he wouldn't even crack a smile. A man to be reckoned with.

Instead the sun was so bright it hurt his now fifty-six year old eyes. He squinted, hoping he looked like Clint Eastwood at least. No, this wasn't at all like he thought it was going to be. It was so bright he could almost imagine a newsperson's camera flash just went off but, as Dave looked around, there was no one, not even his brother let alone the media, came to see him back in society. There was a prison van parked in the shade with a driver to take him to the Greyhound station. "Guess I'm old news," he muttered as he shuffled over to his ride.

"Can I get a lift to downtown?"

"That's what I'm here for. I was told you asked for a ride to town though you kind of seemed like you were expecting someone."

"Well, I wasn't sure if anybody was going to make it. Everybody was pretty busy today but I wanted out anyway. Probably have a party when I get back home."

Dave hadn't gotten many letters while he paid his debt to society. Not a single one from Patti, a couple from his lawyer, about twenty from his ex-cellmate and one from his parent's lawyer when his father passed away. Oh yeah, mom did write a loving, supportive note saying that Dave's legacy to the Ciszek family hastened his father's death. Thanks mom.

Dave's burning desire for revenge wasn't even a warm ember anymore, just an ash, spent a few years back when he realistically thought about finally getting out. What would he do? If he contacted Patti and that assh-ole she married, *if* they were still hitched, he could end up back in Midvale Prison. No, not an option. Dave was not the classic institutionalized per-sonality who couldn't live on the outside and longed to return to the "good life" where he was a big man in the joint.

For one thing, Dave had never been the "man" although he had joined the Aryans for protection in prison. Another was the yearning he had for a woman which had been reaching colossal proportions as his parole date neared. For the first two-thirds of his sentence he had fantasized over Patti, later his dreams became more generic but not more geriatric. Ah, young women, like back in high school.

In his dreams he'd be back in high school, back in his letter jacket and more girls admiring him than he could ever handle at any given time. In those dreams Patti was just one of them vying for his attention, if not a chance for a horizontal bop with the local sports star. Those were the days, my friend....

"We're here, sport," announced the driver.

"Thanks. I've never ridden in such a quiet van before. Time kind of got away from me."

"Well, first off it's a bus, and it's not only totally electric, it totally charges itself."

"Right. I've heard about that even though I'm still not sure how it's possible. I've been in for damn near twenty years. Lots has changed, I guess. Thanks."

"You're welcome. Don't come back."

Dave just shook his head. No, he'd rather die than come back. He bought a ticket back to his hometown with the grubstake the prison had given him and sat down to ponder his future.

The years had been kind to Dave in the way that some people look bet-ter when they've matured. He was in the stage between middle age and before he started to look old. When most people reach the older looking stage, usually between the late fifties and early seventies, they'd appear to change rapidly. Maybe it was genetic or bad health or maybe a life event would beat them down but, whatever, it seemed to happen quickly once it started.

If Dave would wear a long sleeved shirt to cover his prison tattoos, he'd look better than most men his age. If he wore a suit, he'd look downright distinguished, like an established banker or some other sort of business leader. It would be a shame to cover his great build he'd worked for because he was buff, he thought. The new, improved look and toned-down attitude might help him find a new job. The machinists nowadays had to attend school for three years, he'd heard, because of the new technology. So that was probably out.

Whatever he ended up doing, it wouldn't be in his hometown, the place where the headquarters of Techno-Systems was located. Dave had read all about the company on the "view only" computer in his cell. Every cell, all private for the last seven years, had a combination computer/television/mandatory educational program system for each person. Thank you liberals, but it had really benefited Dave and he hadn't been paying taxes to support the program, so, why not?

No, not his hometown where his biggest mistake would be amplified whenever the local media had a slow news day, but he was drawn back nonetheless. Sneak in and sneak out, if possible, then hit the bricks in a bigger city. Before he left though, he wanted to see his family, if they'd see him, and to see what Patti looked like now. Odd, Dave thought, my family is more important to me than that piece of tail that helped land me in stir. Patti might be impressed with the way I look now, or maybe not, being she's loaded and living the good life.

Patti Nelson *was* living the good life except old habits die hard and she still liked to fool around with a variety of men. Her most prominent asset was her net worth rather than the sexy persona she had twenty years ago. That wasn't to say she was unattractive because her face still looked pretty good but her body had taken sort of a hit. The wider hips, once the object of most healthy men's fantasies, looked somewhat grotesque now, especially when she had really slimmed down about five years ago.

Right before Kevin retired, he was heard to comment upon seeing Patti, from the back, sitting on a bench that she "looked like a toilet plunger."

Her pelvic area had splayed out to scary proportions in relative to her upper body. If it had been operable, she would have paid any amount to look normal. In fact, she had spent much of her initially ill-gained funds on cosmetic surgery although her hips, which some thought were from bearing ten to fifteen kids, precluded corrective action. Patti intentionally put on enough weight to help hide the hip thing and wore certain types of clothing.

She'd pick up almost any guy in a pinch, which was happening more and more often now that she was getting a reputation. Luckily for her, many guys, including some of the younger ones, would go to bed with any woman, particularly one who would pick up the check. Besides, Patti had changed although she still looked pretty good for her age. Unlike Dave though, Patti would probably look old all of a sudden when even her cosmetic surgeons couldn't stem the relentless tide of nature.

Bill Nelson had an idea that Patti had gone back to, what he knew now, were her old tricks. He went out of his way to avoid any kind of situation wherein he might catch her with another man and also avoided confronting her with what were the fairly well known facts in their circles. He certainly didn't condone it but was content to maintain their current situation for the sake of the business, Techno-Systems, Inc. Like Patti, Bill hadn't faired as well with the passage of time as much as Dave Ciszek either, but at least he still looked more like the younger Bill, albeit a little older.

Bill's hair was thinner, grayer and, what was left, a little longer. Patti had decided that he would look more successful if he grew longer hair and a well-trimmed beard, as if she really cared other than the obligatory parties and other affairs they attended together for appearance's sake. Bill flat out rejected the hair transplant suggestion and other cosmetic enhancements she thought would look good on him. He just plain didn't care what the opposite sex saw when they looked at him. Never a vain man, he always figured he age the way the good Lord must have wanted him to, right up to the day he'd die.

Both were very well off but where Patti wanted out of the day to day operations of Techno-systems, Bill wanted in for as long as possible, again until the day he died, the good Lord willing. They had installed an experienced President though Bill was a hands-on kind of CEO. He felt it was his mission that Techno-Systems remain a highly ethical company and the relatively new President deferred to Bill in those matters. Bill had also become a devoutly religious person, especially over the last few years, and liked to think that his beliefs were reflected in the way his company conducted business.

Bill was usually confident that his wife would not be part of the group he now preferred to spend his time with, away from Techno-Systems that is. He was totally correct in this assumption because Patti worshipped the financial resources that allowed her the means to live the life she preferred. Bill thought she'd either change in a few years or become pathetically desperate, unable to accept the diminishing returns of cosmetic surgery.

A real downer as Kevin would have said, although Bill could genuinely say that it didn't make too much difference to him as long as he wasn't dragged down with her. Truth be told, he would have bought Patti out if he could've afforded it, but she controlled half the assets. Bill's persistence had waned over the years though his patience was still intact so he'd just wait and see.

Kevin had retired down in Panama City, Panama, where there were so many North Americans that the Panamanians wanted stiffer immigration laws to maintain their culture.

Jeremy was the Director of Manufacturing at Techno-Systems and, like Bill, wanted to stay as long as possible. Older than Kevin at seventy-one, he knew that he was little more than a figurehead now but had paid his dues so Bill agreed to accommodate his wishes in perpetuity.

Bill Sexton had been the first to retire of the original QMT although it had been for medical reasons. The nicest guy at Techno-Systems had had a heart attack just four years after they had gotten their first government contract but he felt good about it because, true to form, Bill took it in stride as a sign. After he left, he went to work for his nephew, William, and worked part-time for him for years. Bill still lived in town and was always welcome at any company event. The last time any of the old gang had seen him had been the twenty-fifth anniversary dinner. Of the entire group, Bill was the happiest and most content with life.

Henry David Thoreau said way back in the 1800s: "The mass of men lead lives of quiet desperation." Though in all fairness he had never met Bill Sexton, who was comfortable in the way he was and his own life the way it happened, unlike most of his old coworkers.

William Sexton was probably the most successful as the owner of a large consulting firm specializing in federal contract management for companies of any size. As a matter of fact, Techno-Systems was one of his accounts although not even in the top three grossing accounts. It was hard to say if his accounts grew with him or if he grew with his accounts but William Sexton had ridden the wave of a half-dozen small businesses that weren't so small anymore, including Techno-Systems.

Techno-Systems, Inc. owed its success to the power of collective imagination and hard work but then the most successful endeavors are ultimately group projects. What started out as Bill Nelson's need for business with longer lead times had grown proportionately with the original team's input to a world class organization. Not any one person was responsible although it could be said that Bill Nelson was the driving force and be partially right because he delegated the initial responsibilities.

The rest of the credit went to all of the other forward thinkers and doers from the first QMT to the entire organization as it was today. Even the people who had come and gone as employees, some only working there for a few days while a few others were lifetime employees, had contributed something, somehow to the success of Techno-Systems.

The reason being was the way the company had always made a conscious effort to *listen* to the employees and *understand* what they were saying. Not everything fell under the category of "pearls of wisdom" from the employees but even farfetched ideas or criticism might have merit if analyzed a little bit. By at least listening to what might be suggested, the employees from top to bottom were usually encouraged to participate because they knew they mattered.

It certainly didn't cost much, and in fact had ultimately been profitable, to allow the entire company to contribute to the well-being of Techno-Systems. Whether the highest paid executive or the newest production associate, the recognition for good ideas and a job well done was equally distributed. Nothing elaborate, just enough to encourage everyone to try and buy into what was best for the company as a whole.

An example was, of the twelve patents that Techno-Systems had been awarded, only two had come from the engineering function, five from management and the rest from production or assembly. Techno-Systems shared some of the profits gained from the patents with the people who made the initial contribution.

An exception to this noble philosophy sat across and down the street from the new headquarters of Techno-Systems, watching the building for familiar faces. Dave Ciszek thought the obviously new construction was nice but it wasn't quite what he expected. World leader, huh? Dave made an estimate of the number of cars parked in the main lot because he had read that the company had a little over three-hundred employees. He gave up when he realized it didn't matter anyway and besides, they probably worked multiple shifts or were highly automated or something.

The only familiar face he was really interested in seeing was Patti's. After a day and a half of not recognizing a single person, Dave checked the telephone listing and found seventeen William Nelsons, narrowed them down by how their houses looked and hit pay dirt the next day. Whoa! Patti still looked mighty fine, at least from a distance, Dave thought, but the front yard was so damned big it was hard to see. He followed her that night to a nice restaurant, staying outside for a couple of hours and then going back to his motel because he wasn't sure if he should approach her.

A strange thing was happening to Dave. Seeing the new manufacturing complex and the fine house Patti lived in was getting him pissed off all over again. While he sat in prison for all that time, both Patti and that ass-hole she married were getting richer. Patti because of the life insurance and the asshole because he ended up not only eliminating the competition, he *married* it! Sonovabitch! Dave decided she owed him. Her asshole husband owed him too.

Patti had told Dave a long time ago that the secret to Bill Nelson's success was his ability to plan what he wanted to do, visualize himself doing it and then, just do it. Great idea, Dave concurred to himself. First part of the plan was to compute how much money they owed him by taking his old pay rate, multiplying it, factoring in a decent annual increase, adding in interest and throwing in something for general principles.

Major bucks, Dave thought but that was only how much *money* they owe me. The madder he became, the more he felt he had coming to him. No, the money was nice but what about not having a woman for all that time? Coincidentally, his cellmate for quite a few years was named Pat. Maybe that was part of what Patti owes me though he didn't know at that point how easy it would be to collect on *that* particular debt now. He was to find out in short order. Only Patti and Dave knew how far their chance reunion years ago had taken them. They had been having a fairly torrid affair for months before he had killed Denny.

"Kill Bill" was one of the movies they had watched together at Dave's apartment during one of their trysts. An option? He had always wondered why she didn't want to be seen with him in public back then. He had also wondered if he hadn't taken the inniative to take out Denny, would she have suggested it? If she had screwed with him, should she die? No, then he'd have nothing to gain besides going back to prison, and probably a maximum security one to boot.

Plan your work and work your plan. Dave started doing just that.

Reference—Websites

The United States Federal Government listing of various agencies could easily fill a book by itself although it would be outdated before the book was printed. It's easier and faster to visit one website:

www.usa.gov

Then click on A-Z Agency Index and select where you want to go. Each agency has links to visit as well.

When in doubt, just enter the subject on your search engine. In the time it takes to lookup a hard copy of the address, you could have clicked your way to a website you know is current.

Reference—Glossary, Acronyms and Abbreviations

Complete dictionaries are available from various governmental websites although the following glossary with the acronyms and abbreviations respectively noted should be adequate. Permission from the Defense Acquisition University (DAU), another great website, was secured to reprint some of their published *Glossary of Defense Acquisition Acronyms & Terms.*

If an acronym's or abbreviation's definition is not self-explanatory enough, try checking the glossary for a more complete description. Please be advised of multiple uses for letters or completely different meanings than standard or generally accepted commercial meanings.

Always make sure you're comfortable with your understanding of what you might be reading or quoting before you finalize anything. Calling your PTAC or SBA before contacting the contracting officer will be time well spent.

An index of subjects by chapters rather than an index for specific page numbers for reference follows the *Glossary, Acronyms and Abbreviations.*

8(a)—An SBA program named for a section of the Small Business Act and developed to assist small businesses compete in the federal marketplace. See the SBA for certification and requirements.

Acquisition—The conceptualization, initiation, design, development, test production, deployment, Logistics Support (LS), modification, and disposal of weapons and other systems, supplies, or services (including construction) to satisfy government needs.

Acquisition Program—A directed, funded effort that provides a new, improved, or continuing material, weapon, or information system or service capability in response to an approved need. Acquisition programs are divided into categories that are established to facilitate decentralized decision making, execution, and compliance with statutory requirements.

Acquisition Streamlining—Any effort that results in a more efficient and effective use of resources to design, develop, or produce quality systems. This includes ensuring that only necessary and cost-effective requirements are included, at the most appropriate time in the acquisition cycle, in solicitations and resulting contracts for the design, development, and production of new systems, or for modifications to existing systems that involve redesign of systems or subsystems.

Activity—A task or measurable amount of work to complete a job or part of a project.

Actual Cost—A cost sustained in fact, on the basis of costs incurred, as distinguished from forecasted or estimated costs.

Actual Cost of Work Performed (ACWP)—The costs actually incurred and recorded in accomplishing the work performed within a given time period.

Administrative Contracting Offices (ACO)—The government Contracting Officer (CO) who is responsible for government contracts administration.

ADP—Automated Data Processing.

Advocates—1. The Office of the Secretary of Defense (OSD) and Services' overseer whose job is to encourage, monitor, enforce, and report progress in attaining certain disciplines and goals. Advocates include competition, streamlining, specifications, and other topical issues. 2. Persons or organizations actively supporting and "selling" an acquisition program.

A/E—Architect/Engineer.

Affordability—A determination that the Life Cycle Cost (LCC) of an acquisition program is in consonance with the long-range investment and force structure plans of the DoD or individual DoD Components.

AI—Artificial Intelligence.

ALC—Air Logistics Center (Air Force).

Analysis of Manufacturing—The review and evaluation of assembly and fabrication processes to determine how effectively and efficiently the contractor's manufacturing operations have been planned or accomplished.

ANSI—American National Standards Institute.

AR—Army Regulation; Acquisition Reform.

Armaments—Weapons with lethal capability (e.g., missiles, rifles).

ASBCA—Armed Services Board of Contract Appeals.

ASPA—Armed Services Procurement Act.

Assembly Chart—Portrays the proposed sequence of assembly operations constituting the assembly process in the production of goods that are composed of many components.

ATP—Acceptance Test Procedures.

Attribute—A quantitative or qualitative characteristic of an element or its actions. (CJCSI 3170.01E)

Audit—Systematic examination of records and documents to determine adequacy and effectiveness of budgeting, accounting, financial, and related policies and procedures; compliance with applicable statutes, regulations, policies, and prescribed procedures; reliability, accuracy, and completeness of financial and administrative records and reports; and the extent to which funds and other resources are properly protected and effectively used.

Authorized Representative—Any person, persons, or board (other than the Contracting Officer (CO) authorized to act for the head of an agency or the Secretary.

Average Procurement Unit Cost (APUC)—APUC is calculated by dividing total procurement cost by the number of articles to be procured. Total procurement cost includes flyaway, rollaway, sail away cost (that is, recurring and nonrecurring costs associated with production of the item such as hardware/software, Systems Engineering (SE), engineering changes and warranties) plus the costs of procuring Technical Data (TD) training, support equipment, and initial spares.

Award—Notification to bidder of acceptance of bid.

BA—Budget Authority; Budget Activity.

Backlog—That known work input that is beyond the workload capability of an organization or segment of an organization for any given period of time.

BAFO—Best and Final Offer.

Ball Park Estimate—Very rough estimate (usually cost estimate), but with some knowledge and confidence. ("somewhere in the ball park.").

Base Year (BY)—A reference period that determines a fixed price level for comparison in economic escalation calculations and cost estimates. The price level index for the BY is 1.000.

Baseline—Defined quantity or quality used as starting point for subsequent efforts and progress measurement that can be technical, cost, or schedule baseline. See Performance Measurement Baseline (PMB) and Acquisition Program Baseline (APB).

Basic Ordering Agreement (BOA)—An instrument of understanding (not a contract) executed between a procuring activity and a contractor, which sets forth negotiated contract clauses that will be applicable to future procurements entered into between the parties during the term of the agreement. It includes as specific a description as possible of the supplies or services and a description of the method for determining pricing, issuing, and delivery of future orders.

BCA—Board of Contract Appeals.

Best Value—The most advantageous trade off between price and performance for the government. Best value is determined through a process that compares strengths, weaknesses, risk, price, and performance, in accordance with selection criteria, to select the most advantageous value to the government.

BOA—Basic Ordering Agreement.

B&P—Bid and Proposal.

Break-even Analysis—1. The study of cost-volume-profit (C-V-P) relationships. 2. The analysis of proposed procurement and facilitization to compare potential costs of establishing a second source with potential savings due to competitive pressure from the second source.

Break-even Point—1. In business enterprises, the point at which revenues from sales exactly equal total incurred cost, I.e., Revenues = Variable

Costs + Fixed Costs. 2. In decision making such as make versus buy, lease versus buy, etc., it is the point of indifference, meaning that level of activity where either method results in exactly the same cost. These types of break-even decisions often involve making assumptions about levels of activity such as number of units needed.

Breakout—Execution of acquisition strategy to convert some parts or system components from contractor furnished to government furnished. Rather than having the prime contractor provide from its sources, the government procures items directly, and provides them to the prime.

Budget—A comprehensive financial plan for the Federal Government, encompassing the totality of federal receipts and outlays (expenditures). Budget documents routinely include the on budget and off budget amounts and combine them to derive a total of federal fiscal activity, with a focus on combined totals. Also a plan of operations for a fiscal period in terms of estimated costs, obligations, and expenditures; source of funds for financing including anticipated reimbursements and other resources; and history and workload data for the projected program and activities.

Burden—Costs that cannot be attributed or assigned to a system as direct cost. An alternative term for Overhead.

Burn-in—The operation of an item under stress to stabilize its characteristics.

Burn Rate—The monthly rate at which a contractor's funds are expended during the period of the contract.

Buy—1. To approve, concur, or accept an action or proposal from another agency or office. 2. The number of end items to be procured either over a certain period or in total.

Buy American Act (BAA)—Provides that the United States Government (USG) generally give preference to domestic end products. (Title 10 U.S. C. & 41 A D). This preference is accorded during the price evaluation process by applying punitive evaluation factors to most foreign products. Subsequently modified (relaxed) by Culver Nunn Amendment (1977) and other 1979 trade agreements for dealing with North Atlantic Treaty Organization (NATO) Allies.

Buy-in—Submission of an offer, usually substantially below estimated costs, with the expectation of winning the contract.

Buy-out—During production when there are multiple contractors, a final competition for the last lot to be produced—winner take all.

BY—Budget Year; Base Year.

CA—Critical Analysis; Commercial Activities; Contract Award.

CAGE Code—Commercial and Government Entity code. 5 Digits.

Calibration—Comparison of an item against a known standard.

CAO—Contract Administration Office.

CAP—Contractor Acquired Property; Critical Acquisition Position.

Capacity Analysis—An analysis most frequently employed in a machine or process area to project capacity for additional business.

CAS—Cost Accounting Standard; Contract Administration Services.

CBD—Commerce Business Daily; Chemical Biological Defense.

CBO—Congressional Budget Office.

CFR—Code of Federal Regulations; Contractor Funds Report.

Change Order (CO)—A unilateral order, signed by a government Contracting Officer (CO), directing the contractor to make a change authorized by the Changes clause without the contractor's consent.

CICA—Competition in Contracting Act (1984).

CID—Commercial Item Description.

Claim—Assertion by one of the contracting parties seeking adjustment or interpretation of an existing contract subject to the dispute clause on the contract.

Clarification—A government communication with an offeror on a competitively negotiated procurement for the sole purpose of eliminating minor irregularities, informalities, or apparent clerical mistakes in a proposal.

CLIN—Contract Line Item Number.

CO—Contracting Officer; Change Order; Commanding Officer.

Commercial Item—A commercial item is any item, other than real property, that is of a type customarily used for nongovernmental purposes and that has been sold, leased, or licensed to the general public; or has been offered for sale, lease, or license to the general public; or any item evolved through advances in technology or performance and that is not yet available in the commercial marketplace in time to satisfy the delivery requirements under a government solicitation. Also included in this definition are services in support of a commercial item, of a type offered and sold competitively in substantial quantities in the commercial marketplace based on established catalog or market prices for specific tasks performed under standard commercial terms and conditions; this does not include services that are sold based on hourly rates without an established catalog or market price for a specified service performed.

Commercial Off-The Shelf (COTS)—Commercial items that require no unique government modifications or maintenance over the life cycle of the product to meet the needs of the procuring agency.

Commodity—A group or range of items that possess similar characteristics, have similar applications, or are susceptible to similar supply management methods.

Competition—An acquisition strategy whereby more than one contractor is sought to bid on a service or function; the winner is selected on the basis of criteria established b y the activity for which the work is to be performed. The law and DoD policy require maximum competition, to the extent possible, throughout the acquisition life cycle.

Competitive Proposals—A procedure used in negotiated procurement that concludes with awarding of a contract to the offeror whose offer is most advantageous to the government.

Competitive Prototyping Strategy (CPS)—Prototype competition between two or more contractors in a comparative side-by-side test.

Component—1. Subsystem, assembly, subassembly, or other major element of an end item. 2. Military Department or agency of the Department of Defense, the Military Departments, the Chairman of the Joint Chiefs of Staff, the combatant commands, the Office of the Inspector General of the Department of Defense, the Defense agencies, DoD field activities, and all other organizational entities within the Department of Defense. (CJCSI3170.01E)

Configuration—A Collection of an item's descriptive and governing characteristics, which can be expressed in functional terms, I.e., what performance the item is expected to achieve; and in physical terms, I.e., what the item should look like and consist of when it is built.

Consumable—Administrative or housekeeping items, general purpose hardware, common tolls, or any item not specifically identified as controlled equipage or spare parts.

Contract—An agreement between two or more legally competent parties, in the proper form, on a legal subject matter or purpose and for legal consideration.

Contract Action—An action resulting in a contract or modification to a contract.

Contract Award—Occurs when the contracting officer has signed and distributed the contract to the contractor.

Contract Categories—There are two broad categories: fixed price contracts and cost-reimbursement contracts. The specific contract types range from Firm-Fixed-Price (FFP), in which the contractor has full responsibility for the performance cost and the resulting profit (loss), to Cost Plus Fixed-Fee (CPFF), in which the contractor has minimal responsibility for the performance cost and the negotiated fee is fixed. In between are various incentive contracts, in which the contractor's responsibility for the performance cost and the profit or fee incentives offered are tailored to the uncertainties involved in contract performance.

Contract Cost Overrun/Under run—A net change in the contractual amount over/under that contemplated by a contract target price, estimated cost plus fee (any type cost reimbursement contract), or red terminable price, due to the contractor's actual contract costs being over/under target or anticipated contracts costs but not attributable to any other cause of cost growth previously defined.

Contract Data Requirements List (CDRL)—A DD Form 1423 list of contract data requirements that are authorized for a specific acquisition and made a part of the contract.

Contract Requirements—In addition to specified performance requirements, contract requirements include those defined in the Statement of

Work (SOW); specifications, standards, and related documents; the Contract Data Requirements List (CDRL); management systems; and contract terms and conditions.

Contract, Cost Plus Fixed-Free CPFF)—A cost reimbursement-type contract that provides for the payment of a fixed fee to the contractor. The fixed fee one negotiated, does not vary with actual cost, but may be adjusted as result of any subsequent changes in the scope of work or services to be performed under the contract.

Contract, Cost Plus Incentive Fee (CPIF)—A cost reimbursement-type contract with provision for a fee, which is adjusted by formula in accordance with the relationship that total allowable costs of contract performance, is designed as an incentive to the contractor to increase the efficiency of performance.

Contract, Cost Plus Percentage of Cost (CPPC)—A form of contract formerly used but now illegal for use by DoD that provided for a fee or profit as a specified percentage of the contractor's actual cost of accomplishing the work to be performed. Sometimes referred to as a "cost plus" or "percentage of cost" contract.

Contract, Cost Reimbursement Type—A type of contract that provides for payment to the contractor of allowable costs incurred in the performance of the contract, to the extent prescribed in the contract. This type of contract establishes an estimate of total cost for the purpose of obligating of funds and establishes a ceiling that the contractor may not exceed without prior approval of the contracting officer. See Contract, Cost Plus Fixed Fee (CPFF) and Contract, Cost Plus Incentive Fee (CPIF).

Contract, Firm-Fixed-Price (FFP)—Provides for a price that is not subject to any adjustment on the basis of the contractor's cost experience in performing the contract. This type of contract places upon the contractor maximum risk and full responsibility for all costs and resulting profit or loss. Provides maximum incentive for the contractor to control costs, and imposes a minimum administrative burden on the government.

Contract, Fixed-Price Incentive Firm (FPIF)—Uses an incentive whereby the contractor's profit is increased or decreased by a predetermined share of an overrun or under run. A firm target is established from which to later compute the overrun or under run. A ceiling price is set as the maximum amount the government will pay. Necessary elements for this type of contract are: target cost—best estimate of expected cost; target profit—fair profit at target cost; share ratio(s)—to adjust profit after actual costs are documented; and, ceiling price—limit the government will pay.

Contract, Fixed Price Type—A type of contract that provides for a firm price to the government, or in appropriate cases, an adjustable price. See Contract, Firm-Fixed-Price (FFP) and Contract, Fixed-Price Incentive Firm (FPIF).

Contract, Fixed rice with Economic Price Adjustment (FPEPA)—A type of contract providing for upward or downward revision of the stated contract price upon the occurrence of a specified contingency. Adjustments may reflect increases/decreases in actual costs of labor or material, or in specific indices of labor or material costs.

Contracting Offices (CO)—A person with authority to enter into, administer, and/or terminate contracts and make related determinations and findings for the United States Government (USG).

Contractor—An entity in private industry which enters into contracts with the government to provide goods or services. In this Glossary the word also applies to government-operated activities that perform work on acquisition defense programs.

Contractor Owned, Contractor Operated (COCO)—A manufacturing facility owned and operated by a private contractor performing a service, under contract, for the government.

Contractor Performance Reporting—Method requiring periodic accounting and reporting by the contractor on performance under contract to date.

Contractual Data Requirement (CDR)—A requirement, identified in a solicitation and imposed in a contract or order, that addresses any aspect of data (I.e., that portion of contractual tasking requirement associated with the development, generation, preparation, modification, maintenance, storage, retrieval, and/or delivery of data).

COR—Contracting Officer's Representative.

Corrective Action—Documented design, process, procedure, or materials changes validated and implemented to correct the cause of failure or design deficiency.

Cost Analysis—An analysis and evaluation of each element of cost in a contractor's proposal to determine reasonableness.

Cost Effectiveness—A measure of the operational capability added by a system as a function of its Life Cycle Cost (LCC).

Cost Estimating Methodologies—1) Comparison/analogy. 2) Parametric. 3) Detailed engineering/bottoms up. 4) Extrapolation from actuals.

COTR—Contracting Officer's Technical Representative.

COTS—Commercial Off-The-Shelf.

CP—Change Proposal.

CPC—Corrosion Prevention and Control.

C/PD—Cost/Pricing Data.

CPFF—Cost Plus Fixed-Fee.

CPI—Critical Program Information; Cost Performance Index; Consumer Price Index.

CPIF—Cost Plus Incentive-Fee.

CPPC—Cost Plus Percentage-of-Cost.

CPR—Contract Performance Report.

Critical Application Item—An item that is essential to weapon system performance or operation, the preservation of life, or the safety of personnel as determined by the military services.

CTP—Critical Technical Parameter.

CV—Cost Variance.

C V P—Cost Volume Profit.

CY—Calendar Year; Current Year.

DA—Department of the Army; Developing Agency; Design Activity.

DAB—Defense Acquisition Board.

DAF—Department of the Air Force.

Data—1. Contracting: All recorded information, regardless of form or characteristic, delivered under contract. Technical Data (TD) exclude management and financial data. (See Limited Rights and Unlimited

Rights.) 2. Software: A representation of facts, concepts, or instruction in a manner suitable for communication, interpretation, or processing by humans or by automation means.

DCAA—Defense Contract Audit Agency.

DCADS—Defense Contracting Action Data System.

DCAS—Defense Contract Administration Services.

DCMA—Defense Contract Management Agency.

Defective Pricing—Result of Cost/Pricing Data (C/PD) that was certified by a contractor to be accurate, current, and complete, but was not.

DESC—Defense Electronic Supply Center.

DFARS—Defense Federal Acquisition Regulation Supplement.

DFAS—Defense Finance and Accounting Service.

DID—Data Item Description.

Direct Cost—Any cost specifically identified with a particular final cost objective. Is not necessarily limited to items that are incorporated into the end product as labor or material.

Direct Labor—Labor specifically identified with a particular final cost objective. Manufacturing direct labor includes fabrication, assembly, inspection, and test for constructing the end product. Engineering direct labor consists of engineering labors such as reliability, Quality Assurance (QA), test, design, etc., that are readily identified with the end product.

Direct Materials—Includes raw materials, purchased parts, and subcontracted items required to manufacture and assembly completed products. A direct material cost is the cost of material used in making a product.

DoC—Department of Commerce.

DoD—Department of Defense.

DoE—Department of Energy.

DON—Department of the Navy.

EAC—Estimate at Completion (Cost).

ECC—Estimated Construction Cost.

ECD—Estimated Completion Date.

Effective Competition—A marketplace condition that results when two or more manufacturing sources are acting independently of each other.

EIS—Environmental Impact Statement.

End Item—The final production product when assembled, or completed, and ready for issue or deployment.

EOM—End of Month.

EOY—End of Year.

EPA—Environmental Protection Agency; Economic Price Adjustment.

ETR—Estimated Time to Repair.

FAR—Federal Acquisition Regulation.

FARA—Federal Acquisition Reform Act (1996).

FASA—Federal Acquisition Streamlining Act (1994).

FAT—First Article Testing; Factory Acceptance Test.

FC—Fixed Cost.

FFF Form Fit Function (or **F3**).

Float—The period of time that an activity may be delayed without becoming a critical activity.

First Article—First article includes preproduction models, initial production samples, test samples, first lots, pilot models, and pilot lots; and approval involves testing and evaluating the first article for conformance with specified contract requirements before or in the initial stage of production under a contract.

Fiscal Year (FY)—For the United States Government (USG), the period covering 1 October to 30 September (12 months).

Fixed Costs—Costs that do not vary with the volume of business, such as property taxes, insurance, depreciation, security, and minimum water and utility fees.

FM—Financial Management.

FOIA—Freedom of Information Act (or **FoIA**).

Form, Fit, and Function (F3) Data—Technical Data (TD) pertaining to items, components, or processes for the purpose of identifying source, size, configuration, mating and attachment characteristics, functional characteristics, and performance requirements.

FOUO—For Official Use Only.

FPAF—Fixed Price Award-Fee.

FPEPA—Fixed Price with Economic Price Adjustment.
FPI—Fixed Price Incentive.
FPIC—Fixed Price Incentive Contract.
FPIF—Fixed Price Incentive Firm.
FPIS—Fixed Price Incentive (Successive Target).
FPR—Final Proposal Revision.
FSC—Federal Supply Code.
FSCM—Federal Supply Code for Manufacturers.
FSG—Federal Stock Group.
FSN—Federal Stock Number.
FY—Fiscal Year.

G&A—General and Administrative.
GAO—Government Accountability Office.
GAT—Government Acceptance Test.
GBL—Government Bill of Lading.
GFE—Government Furnished Equipment.
GFF—Government Furnished Facilities.
GFI—Government Furnished Information.
GFM—Government Furnished Material.
GFP—Government Furnished Property.
GFS—Government Furnished Software.
Given—A premise, fact, or assumption generally universally accepted at the outset.
Goods—Any articles, materials, supplies, or manufactured products, including inspection and test equipment. The term excludes Technical Data (TD).
GS—General Schedule.
GSA—General Services Administration.

HAZCOM—Hazard Communication.
HAZMAT—Hazardous Material.
HQ—Headquarters.

ICA—Independent Cost Analysis.

ICP—Inventory Control Point.

IDDQ—Indefinite Delivery Definite Quantity.

IDIQ—Indefinite Delivery Indefinite Quantity.

IFB—Invitation for Bid.

In Process Inventory Control—The process whereby materials and parts are efficiently planned and controlled to assure their availability at the required stage of production.

Incentive—Motivating the contractor in calculable monetary terms to turn out a product that meets significantly advanced performance goals, to improve on the contract schedule up to and including final delivery, to substantially reduce costs of the work, or to complete the project under a weighted combination of some or all of these objectives.

Indefinite Quantity Contract (IQC)—Provides for furnishing an indefinite quantity, within stated limits, of specific supplies or services, during a specified contract period, with deliveries to be scheduled by the timely placement of orders upon the contractor by activities designed either specifically or by class.

Industry—The defense industry (private sector contractors) includes large and small organizations providing goods and services to DoD. Their perspective is to represent interests of the owners or stockholders.

Inspection—Visual examination of the item (hardware and software) and associated descriptive documentation, which compares appropriate characteristics with predetermined standards to determine conformance to requirements without the use of special laboratory equipment or procedures.

Intellectual Property—Includes inventions, trademarks, patents, industrial designs, copyrights, and technical information including software, data designs, technical know-how, manufacturing information and know-how techniques, Technical Data Packages (TDPs), manufacturing data packages, and trade secrets.

Internal Audit—The independent appraisal activity within an organization for the review of the accounting, financial, and related operations as a basis for protective and constructive services to management.

Invitation for Bid (IFB)—A solicitation document used in sealed bidding.

IQC—Indefinite Quantity Contract.

Issue—Something in dispute or to be decided.

JA—Job Analysis.

JEDMICS—Joint Engineering Data Management Information Control System.

JIT—Just in Time.

JO—Job Order.

Job Shop—A manufacturing enterprise devoted to producing special or custom made parts of products usually in small quantities for specific customers.

K—Contract.

KO—Contracting Officer (also **CO**).

Labor Standards—A compilation by time study of standard time for each element of a given type of work.

Local Purchase—Authorized purchase of materials, supplies, and services by a DoD organization from local commercial sources.

Maintenance—Action necessary to retain or restore an item to a specified condition. See Preventive Maintenance, Corrective Maintenance, Event Maintenance, Scheduled Maintenance, and unscheduled Maintenance.

Manufacturer—Typically, a company that produces a product. Manufacturers are normally also vendors. See Vendor.

MAS—Military Agency for Standardization.

Material Specification—This type of specification is applicable to raw material (chemical compound) mixtures (cleaning agents, paints), or semi-fabricated material (electrical cable, copper tubing) used in the fabrication of a product. Normally, a material specification applies to production but may be prepared to control the development of a material.

MILSCAP—Military Standard Contract Administration Procedure.

MILSPEC—Military Specification.
MILSTD—Military Standard.
Mission—The objective or task, together with the purpose, which clearly indicates the action to be taken.
Mission Need—A statement of operational capability required to perform an assigned mission or to correct a deficiency in existing capability to perform the mission.
MOA—Memorandum of Agreement.
MOE—Measure of Effectiveness.
MOP—Measure of Performance.
MOS—Measure of Suitability.
MSDS—Material Safety Data Sheet.
MYP—Multiyear Procurement.

NAICS—North American Industry Class System.
NAS—National Aerospace Standard.
NASA—National Aeronautics and Space Administration.
NCC—Negotiated Contract Cost.
Negotiated Contract—One obtained by direct agreement with a contractor without sealed bids.
Negotiation—Contracting through the use of either competitive or other-than-competitive proposals and discussions. Any contract awarded without using sealed bidding procedures is a negotiated contract.
Nomenclature—Set or system of official names or titles given to items of material or equipment.
NOI—Notice of Intent.
NRC—Nonrecurring Cost.
NSN—National Stock Number.
NTE—Not to Exceed.
NWC—National War College; Navy War College; Nuclear Weapons Council; Nuclear Weapons Center.

OB—Operating Budget.

Obligation—A duty to make a future payment of money. The duty is incurred as soon as an order is placed, or a contract is awarded for the delivery of goods and the performance of services. The placement of an order is sufficient. An obligation "legally" encumbers a specified sum of money, which will require outlay (s) or expenditures in the future.

Offer—A response to a solicitation that, if accepted, would bind the offeror to perform the resultant contract.

Off-the-Shelf—Procurement of existing systems or equipment without a Research, Development, Test and Evaluation ((RDT&E) program or with minor development necessary to made system suitable for DoD needs. May be commercial system/equipment or one already in DoD inventory. See Commercial Item (CI) and Non-Developmental Item (NDI).

OMB—Office of Management and Budget.

Option—A contractual clause permitting an increase in the quantity of supplies beyond that originally stipulated or an extension in the time for which services on a time basis may be required.

Ordering Activity—An activity that originates a requisition or order for procurement, production, or performance of work or services by another activity.

Packaging—The process and procedures used to protect material. It includes cleaning, drying, preserving, packing, and unitization.

Packing, Handling, Storage, and Transportation (PHST)—The resources, processes, procedures, design considerations, and methods to ensure all system, equipment, and support items are preserved, packaged, handled, and transported properly. This includes environmental considerations, equipment preservation requirements for short-and long-term storage, and transportability. One of the traditional Logistics Support (LS) elements.

P/B—Program/Budget.

PBA—Performance Based Acquisition.

PCO—Procuring Contracting Officer.

Performance—Those operational and support characteristics of the system that allow it to effectively and efficiently perform its assigned mission over time. The support characteristics of the system include both support-ability aspects of the design and the support elements necessary for system operation.

PM—Program Manager; Project Manager; Product Manager.

PO—Program Office; Purchase Order; Project Order; Purchasing Office.

Point of Contact (POC)—Person serving as coordinator, action officer, or focal point for an activity.

PR—Procurement Request; Purchase Request; Public Relations.

PRA—Paper Reduction Act.

Preaward Survey (Facility Capability Review)—Study of financial, organizational, and operational status made prior to contract award to determine a prospective contractor's responsibility and eligibility for government procurement.

Prime Contract—A contract agreement or purchase order entered into by a contractor with the government.

Prime Contractor—The entity with whom an agent of the United States enters into a prime contract for the purposes of obtaining supplies, materials, equipment, or service of any kind.

Process—1. The combination of people, equipment, materials, methods, and environment that produces output—a given product or service. A process can involve any aspect of a business. 2. A key tool for managing processes is statistical process control, a planned series of actions of operations that advances a material or procedure from one stage of completion to another. #. A planned and controlled treatment that subjects materials to the influence of one or more types of energy for the time required to bring about the desired reactions or results.

Procurement—Act of buying goods and services for the government.

Procurement Data Package (PDP)—Includes documentation prepared expressly for the identification description, and verification of items, materials, supplies, and services that are to be purchased, inspected, packaged, packed and supplied, or delivered to users.

Procurement (Local)—Procurement of material or services by an installation or its satellite activities or smaller stations. Such procurement overseas is by a military command for consumption within the command area. (Distinguished from central procurement).

Procuring Contracting Officer (PCO)—The individual authorized to enter into contracts for supplies and services on behalf of the government by sealed bids or negotiations, and who is responsible for overall procurement under the contract.

Product—1. The result of Research, Development, Test and Evaluation (RDT&E) in terms of hardware or software being produced (manufactured). Also Known as an end item. 2. The item stipulated in a contract to be delivered under the contract (I.e., service, study, or hardware).

Profit—The excess amount realized from the sales of goods over the cost thereof in a given transaction or over a given period.

Progress Payments—Payments made to a prime contractor during the life of a fixed-price type contract on the basis of a percentage of incurred total costs or total direct labor and material costs.

Proprietary Right—A broad contractor term used to describe data belonging to the contractor. These data could be intellectual property, financial data, etc. This is generally a term used in the submission of a proposal to protect the contractor's sensitive information from disclosure and is not a category of rights applicable to Technical Data (TD) under all contracts.

Protest—A concern over the award of a contract, submitted to Government Accountability Office (GAO) or Procuring Contracting Office (PCO).

PTAC—Procurement Technical Assistance Center.

PTAP—Procurement Technical Assistance Program.

Purchase Order (PO)—A contractual procurement document used primarily to procure supplies and no personal services when the aggregate amount involved in any one transaction is relatively small (e.g., not exceeding 25,000).

QBL—Qualified Bidders List.

Qualification—The formal process by which a manufacturer's product is examined for compliance with the requirements of a source control drawing for the purpose of approving the manufacturer as a source of supply.

Quality—The composite of material attributes including performance features and characteristics of a production or service to satisfy a customer's given need.

Quality Assurance (QA)—A planned and systematic pattern of all actions necessary to provide confidence that adequate technical requirements are established, that products and services conform to established technical requirements, and that satisfactory performance is achieved.

Quality Control (QC)—The system or procedure used to check product quality throughout the acquisition process.

Raw Materials—Includes raw and processed material in a form or state that requires further processing.

RC—Reserve Component.

Repair—The restoration or replacement of parts or components of real property or equipment as necessitated by wear and tear, damage, failure of parts or the like, in order to maintain it in efficient operating condition.

Request for Proposal (RFP)—A solicitation used in negotiated acquisition to communicate government requirements to prospective contractor and to solicit proposals.

Request for Quotation (RFQ)—A solicitation used in negotiated acquisition to communicate government requirements to prospective contractors and to solicit a quotation. A response to an RFQ is not an offer; however, it is informational in character.

Request for Technical Proposal (RTP)—Solicitation document used in two-step sealed bid. Normally in letter form, it asks only for technical information—price and cost breakdowns are forbidden.

Review—The discrete process of gathering and evaluating information to make a decision about a program. Examples are milestone reviews and other program decision reviews.

Rework—Any corrections of defective work, either before, during or after inspection.

RFB—Request for Bid.

RFI—Ready for Issue; Request for Information.

RFP—Request for Proposal.

RFQ—Request for Quotation.

Rights in Technical Data (TD)—The right for the government to acquire TD. If the government has funded or will fund a part of or the entire development of the item, component or process, then the government is entitled to unlimited rights in the TD. However, if the above is developed by a contractor or subcontractor exclusively at private expense, the government is entitled to limited rights. Such data must be unpublished and identified as limited rights data. See Limited Rights, Government Purpose License Rights, and Unlimited Rights.

Risk—A measure of the inability to achieve program objectives within defined cost and schedule constraints. Risk is associated with all aspects of the program, e. g., threat, technology, design processes, or Work Breakdown Structure (WBS) elements. It has two components: the probability of failing to achieve a particular outcome, and the consequences of failing to achieve that outcome.

RTP—Request for Technical Proposal.

SADBU—Small and Disadvantaged Business Utilization.

SBA—Small Business Administration; Simulation Based Acquisition.

SBIR—Small Business Innovation Research (Program).

SCN—Specification Change Notice; Shipbuilding and Conversion, Navy(Appropriation); Software Change Notice.

SDB—Small Disadvantaged Business.

SDBUP—Small Disadvantaged Business Utilization Program.

SIC—Standard Industrial Classification—See **NAICS.**

Sole Source Acquisition—A contract for the purchase of supplies or services that is entered into or proposed to be entered into by an agency after soliciting and negotiating with only one source.

Solicitation—In contracting, the term means to go out to prospective bidders and request their response to a proposal.

SOO—Statement of Objectives.

SOW—Statement of Work.

SPC—Statistical Process Control.

Spare Parts—Repairable components or assemblies used for maintenance replacement purposes in major end items of equipment.

SPEC—Specification.

Special Tooling (ST)—All jigs, dies, fixtures, molds, patterns, taps, gauges, other equipment and manufacturing aids, and replacements thereof, which are of specialized nature that, without substantial modification or alteration, their use is limited to the development or production of particular services.

SSP—Source Selection Plan.

ST—Special Tooling.

Standard—In work measurement, any established or accepted rule, model, or criterion against which comparisons are made.

Standard Industrial Classification (SIC) Code—An industrial classification method used to report price index changes. A code number is assigned to specific industry groups.

Statement of Objectives (SOO)—That portion of a contract that establishes a broad description of the government's required performance objectives.

Statement of Work (SOW)—That portion of a contract that establishes and defines all no specification requirements for contractor's efforts either directly or with the use of specific cited documents.

Subcontract—A contract or contractual action entered into by a prime contractor or subcontractor for the purpose of obtaining supplies, materials, equipment, or services under a prime contract.

Subcontractor—A contractor who enters into a contract with a prime contractor.

Supplies—All property except land or interest in land. Includes, but is not limited to, public works, facilities, ships, aircraft, machine tools, and their parts and accessories.

Supply—The procurement, distribution, maintenance while in storage, and salvage of supplies, including the determination of kind and quantity of supplies. The Producer Phase extends from determination of procurement schedules to acceptance of finished supplies by the military services. The Consumer Phase extends from receipt of finished supplies by the military services through issue for use or consumption.

Support Item—An item that is used to support an end item (e.g., a tool, a piece of test equipment, or a training device).

TAAF—Test, Analyze and fix.

TACOM—Tank-automotive and Armaments Command Army).

TAT—Turn Around Time.

TBD—To be Determined or Developed.

TC—Type Classification.

TCO—Termination Contracting Officer.

TD—Test Director; Technical Data; Technical Director; Technology Development.

TDP—Technical Data Package; Test Design Plan.

TDR—Technical Data Rights.

T&E—Test and Evaluation.

TE—Test Equipment.

Teaming—An agreement of two or more firms to form a partnership or joint venture to act as a potential prime contractor; or an agreement by a potential prime contractor to act as a subcontractor under a specified acquisition program; or an agreement for a joint proposal resulting from a normal prime contractor-subcontractor, licensee-licenser, or leader company relationship.

Technical Data (TD)—Scientific or technical information recorded in any form or medium (such as manuals and drawings) necessary to operate and maintain a defense system. Documentation of computer programs and related software are TD. Computer programs and related software are not TD. Also excluded are financial data or other information related to contract administration. One of the traditional elements of Logistics Support (LS).

Technical Data Package (TDP)—A technical description of an item adequate for supporting an acquisition strategy, production, engineering, and Logistics Support (LS). The description defines the required design configuration and procedures to ensure adequacy of item performance. It consists of all applicable TD such as drawings, associated lists, specifications, standards, performance requirements, Quality Assurance (QA) provisions, and packaging details. One of the traditional LS elements.

TFC—Termination for Convenience.

TFD—Termination for Default.

Tiering—Formerly, specifications and standards referenced in a contract that, within themselves, reference other documents that reference still more documents, etc. This practice was formally stopped by the Secretary of Defense (SECDEF) in a 1994 memorandum.

TINA—Truth in Negotiation Act.

TL—Termination Liability.

TLS—Time Line Sheet.

TM—Technical Manual; Technical Management.

TMDE—Test, Measurement and Diagnostic Equipment.

TO—Technical Order.

Total Quality Management (TQM)—A management philosophy committed to a focus on continuous improvements of product and services with the involvement of the entire workforce.

TQM—Total Quality Management.

TRD—Technical Requirements Document.

Two-Step Sealed Bids—A method of procurement that combines competitive procedures in order to obtain the benefits of sealed bidding when adequate specifications are not available. In step one, firms are allowed to submit technical (not price) proposals to satisfy a requirement. In step two, each firm with a satisfactory technical approach is then allowed to submit a sealed bid (price), which used that firm's approach as the contract specification. Award goes to the low responsive and responsible bidder. Formerly called Two-Step formal Advertising.

UCF—Uniform Contract Format.

UCR—Unit Cost Report.

UID—Unique Identification.

UPS—Uniform Procurement System.

Undefinitized Contract Action (UCA)—Any contract action for which the terms, specifications, or price are not agreed upon before performance is begun under the action. Examples are letter contracts, orders under basic ordering agreements, and provisioned item orders, for which the price has not been agreed upon before performance has begun. Letter contracts await negotiation to definitive prices (DFARS 217.7401 (d).

Unique Identification (UD)—Unique identification is the set of data that uniquely marks any tangible asset, for example, an item, component, sub-system, or system. UID data are globally unique and unambiguous, ensure data integrity and data quality throughout the life of the item, and support multifaceted business applications and users.

United State Code (U.S.C.)—A consolidation and codification of the general and permanent laws of the United States arranged according to subject matter under 50 title headings, in alphabetical order to a large degree. Sets out the current status of the laws, as amended. Title 10 governs the Armed Forces.

Unsolicited Proposal—A written proposal that is submitted to any agency on the submitter's initiative for the purpose of obtaining a contract with the government, and which is not in response to a formal or informal request.

USAF—United States Air Force.

U.S.C.—United States Code.

USCG—United States Coast Guard.

USG—United States Government.

USMC—United States Marine Corps.

USN—United States Navy.

VC—Variable Cost.

VE—Value Engineering.

Vendor—An individual, partnership, corporation, or other activity that sells property, goods, or services. A vendor may supply a government contractor. Vendors may be manufacturers, that is, actually produce the product or service they sell, or not. For example, a company that buys personal computers from a computer manufacturer under a contract name and then sells them to the government is a vendor (to the government) but not a manufacturer.

Waiver—1. Specifications. A written authorization to accept a Configuration Item (CI) or other designated item, which, during production, or after having been submitted for inspection is found to depart from specified requirements, but nevertheless is considered suitable "as is" or after rework by an approved method. 2. Decision to not require certain criteria to be met for certain reasons, such as national security.

Warranty—A promise or affirmation given by a contractor to the government regarding the nature, usefulness, or condition of the supplies or performance of services furnished under a contract.

WBS—Work Breakdown Structure.

Weighted Guidelines—A government technique for developing fee and profit negotiation objectives, within percentage ranges established by regulation.

Win-Win—A philosophy whereby all parties in a defense acquisition scenario come away gaining some or most of what they wanted (I.e., everyone "wins" something, even though it may not be 100 percent of the goal): the ideal outcome.

WIP—Work in Place.

WOSB—Woman-Owned Small Business.

Reference—Index of Subjects by Chapter

The names of the chapters say a lot about their contents although the highlights and other unrelated subjects are listed as well. This book's intent is to pique your curiosity about government contracting and to give you a basic understanding of the process, good and bad, in a more interesting format than usual. Other sources can provide more detailed reference if necessary.

Chapter 1. The Story

- Why and When to pursue Government Contracts

- Goals vs. Plans

- Prospecting Methods

Chapter 2. Getting Started

- How Big is the Government Marketplace

- Misconceptions

- PTAC and SBA

- Mission Statement suggestions

Chapter 3. Getting Registered

- What do I need for CCR Registration

- Checklist

Chapter 4. Quality Assurance

- FAR requirements

- Specs—outdated but still referenced

- ISO benefits

Chapter 5. ISO 9001:2000

- Steps

- Sample Quality Manual

- Quality management principles

- Quality Policy suggestions

- Internal Audits

Chapter 6. The SBA

- Basics

- HUBZone

Chapter 7. Finding Opportunities

- FedBizOpps

- How to search the FBO

- The Contracting Officer

- Commercial Accounts as Subcontractors

- Subcontracting Examples and Checklist

Chapter 8. Reviewing Requests

- Numbered Notes

978-0-595-44921-7
0-595-44921-2

www.ingramcontent.com/pod-product-compliance
Lightning Source LLC
Chambersburg PA
CBHW030926180526
45163CB00002B/479